Life in Britain since 1700

Peter and Mary Speed

Oxford University Press 1982

Oxford University Press, Walton Street, Oxford OX2 6DP

London Glasgow New York Toronto
Delhi Bombay Calcutta Madras Karachi
Nairobi Dar es Salaam Salisbury Cape Town
Kuala Lumpur Singapore Hong Kong Tokyo
Melbourne Auckland

and associate companies in
Beirut Berlin Ibadan Mexico City

© Oxford University Press 1982

ISBN 0 19 913282 8

All rights reserved. No part of this publication may be reproduced, stored in a retrieval system, or transmitted, in any form, or by any means electronic, mechanical, photocopying, recording, or otherwise, without the prior permission of Oxford University Press.

This book is sold subject to the condition that it shall not, by way of trade or otherwise, be lent, re-sold, hired or otherwise, circulated without the publisher's prior consent in any form of binding or cover other than that in which it is published and without a similar condition including this condition being imposed on the subsequent purchaser.

Phototypeset by Western Printing Services Ltd, Bristol
Printed in Hong Kong

Contents

1	Homes and Families	*4*
2	Leisure	*16*
3	Education	*28*
4	The Care of the Poor	*40*
5	Law and Order	*52*
6	Medicine	*64*
7	Inland Transport	*76*
8	Sea and Air Transport	*88*
9	The Countryside	*100*
10	Industry	*112*

1 Homes and Families

Homes and Families in the Eighteenth Century

Homes. The picture below shows a stately home that was built in the eighteenth century. You may have visited one like it. At that time it was the fashion to make important buildings look as much as possible like those of Greece and Rome. You can see how well they succeeded.

No expense was spared on these elegant houses, but if we had lived in them we would not have found it comfortable. There was no central heating, and usually there was no bathroom or indoor lavatory.

The houses of ordinary people were not in any particular style. Folk just built what they needed, with local materials and employed the same methods that had been used for generations. There were some changes though. For example the hall had once been the centre of family life and all the cooking and baking had been done there. Now many houses had a second room, with a fireplace for some of the cooking. This was later to become the kitchen.

Families. Rich people or people in business did not allow their children to marry for love. Marriage was a business arrangement that would bring some advantage to the family as a whole. Their idea of the family was much wider than ours. A landowner would think of the generations that would come after him. The farmer or the business man would include his apprentices and his servants in his family. They all lived and worked with his wife and children.

The rich man's wife had one important task, which was to bear a son to inherit the family estate. A man in business needed his wife as a full working partner. She was expected to earn her own keep and a good deal more as well. Neither of these women was a housewife. The one was too grand and the other was too busy with more important things. Both left the care of the house and small children to the servants.

Rich parents were glad to have children. Indeed,

Chiswick House, designed by the Earl of Burlington, 1725

An Elizabethan house, Charlecote Manor. Note the large windows and chimneys.

it was a disaster for them if they did not have a son. Apart from the eldest son, though, the others could cause worry and expense. In a working household children were welcome for the help they gave and the money they earned. Both little boys and girls were soon set to work at anything they could do, often for many hours in the day. Childhood, as a time for play, was very brief.

Many babies and young children, including those born to wealthy families, died because there was no medical care as we know it today.

The eighteenth-century squire

My new house has just been finished and I am more than pleased with it. The cost was high, but as it took twenty-five years to complete, I have been able to find the money out of my income without too much difficulty.

The house is, of course, in the correct Palladian style. My architect copied some designs of Mr. William Kent, so he made sure of that. We have had classical buildings of a kind in England for a long time now. My old house had classical type orders around its main entrance and its fireplaces. But when I went on my Grand Tour, I saw the true Roman buildings in Italy, and I saw also how well the Italians had brought the classical tradition back to life. I was determined to do the same in England.

I have chosen to use the Doric Order for I like its simple lines. You can be sure that all my columns and pilasters are correct in every detail. One of the worst mistakes of the old builders was to mix classical details with rather old fashioned English features. I understand that in the days of Queen Elizabeth a man was proud if he could afford glass, so he made his windows as large as possible. But if a house is to look elegant, then the windows should be of the proper size and properly spaced. I regret that I must have chimneys. They are most unclassical, but in our climate we have no choice. Still, my architect has kept them out of sight as much as possible.

For a jest, my architect asked me if I would like a bathroom, as some of the great nobles are having. This I refused. We have washstands in all the bedrooms, and if anyone must have a bath, a servant can bring him a tub. A bathroom would be quite unnecessary. It would seem there is also some

A squire's family. Adults and children dressed alike in those days.

This dressing room, in the Chinese style, was also the bathroom!

new fangled device called a water closet. Where is the point of that when you can use a chamber pot at night and a good privy in the garden during the day?

I have a wife and six children, two sons and four daughters. We buried two other children who died from the smallpox. My parents insisted that I should marry sensibly—not that I needed much persuasion. My wife's father had no sons and when he died she inherited a large share of his estate. This added to my own, gives us a fair income.

My sons were educated at home by private tutors, and then went to Oxford. The older one will inherit the estate, of course. The younger boy is still at Oxford and he is undecided about his future. I may buy him a commission in the Guards, or perhaps a living in the Church. Naturally there is no question of him inheriting any of the estate. That must never be divided. In my will I have forbidden my son to sell any land. That is to make sure the estate passes intact to my grandson, and continues in the family. Thanks to my own marriage and the purchases I have made, I own a great deal of land. I trust my family fortunes will continue to grow. I am a Justice of the Peace, and well known in this county. Possibly, my grandson will become a peer, with a seat in the House of Lords and be able to buy his own son a seat in the House of Commons.

My daughters need less education than my sons. We have a governess who teaches them writing, French and Italian. A dancing master and a music master instruct them once a week. A lady must be accomplished, but she must never try to be superior to any man she may meet in society. Daughters are a serious problem. It is unthinkable that they should not marry, but when they do each must have a dowry that is large enough to match my good name in the county. But it is difficult to find the money without borrowing heavily, or, worse, selling some of my land.

A Yorkshire clothier

I am a clothier. That means I make woollen cloth. I also have a small farm, which produces food for my family, and enough left over to sell.

When you first enter my house you come into the hall. We have no money for fancy ornaments, but it answers well. There is a floor of flagstones and a fireplace. Here we do most of our cooking. We have an iron kettle, a couple of iron cooking pots, a pan and a spit for roasting.

There is a good wooden table, big enough to seat the whole family including the woman servant and the apprentice. Off the hall at one end there is a chamber where my wife and I sleep. It has a feather bed and a chest for linen. At the other end of the hall there is a room with its own hearth and an oven. This is where we bake our bread and brew our beer. Upstairs there are two chambers. There is a small one for my daughter and the woman servant. My sons and my apprentice sleep in the larger of the two, but the main use of that is for weaving. We have three looms, so there is little enough room for beds. In truth, we all have very little time for sleeping.

Outside is the yard, with its pump, and grouped round it the farm buildings—a small barn, a cow house, a stable and a dairy.

My family is my wife, Ann, my daughter, my three sons, an apprentice and a woman servant. Until last year my mother also lived with us but for several years she had been too old and infirm to help with the work of the household. My daughter is fifteen, one son is ten, another six, and the third is a baby. My wife has a baby almost every year, well, say two in every three years. Many of them have died in infancy. I think we have buried six. Our neighbours say we are lucky to have three, and seem likely to rear a fourth. Children can be useful in many ways. My daughter is to be married soon. She says she doesn't like the young man, but I will have none of her nonsense. He is the son of a grazier who supplies me with much of my wool, so the marriage will be good for business. I hope that

Taking cloth to market by pack-horse. In what ways do you think this was inefficient?

In the Yorkshire clothier's family, spinning was women's work while the men were the weavers.

soon my sons will be able to help more on the farm. They are not strong enough for that yet, but at their age they are too old for play and we find them plenty to do. They unwind the fleeces, and take out any stones or dirt that might have got in by mistake. They can help wash the wool, and the older boy is quite good at carding, or combing the wool. There are plenty of jobs for them in the house, such as fetching wood, drawing water, sweeping floors and minding the baby.

The most important part of my work is buying fleeces from the graziers and selling my finished cloth. We deliver it by pack-horse to the cloth hall at Bradford. All that takes me about a day. Then, together with my apprentice, I do the work on the farm that is too heavy for the women, such as the ploughing, the muck spreading and the reaping. There are seasons of the year when I do little but farm work. Most of the time, though, I spend at my loom. We live by the sale of our cloth, so weaving is of the first importance.

Looking after the house is the work of the female servant. She cooks the meals, washes the linen, sweeps the floors, does such cleaning as we need, and cares for the baby. My sons help her, as I have explained, so I will not allow her to spend too long on such trivial work. She is needed to help the other women for much of the day.

Neither my wife nor my daughter has a minute in which to play the lady. They expect to earn their own keep and more besides. Our cows have to be milked, and that is only the start of it, for their milk must be turned into cheese, or the cream skimmed to make butter. The pigs need to be fed, as do the poultry. Then they have a large garden to tend, where they grow all the vegetables we need. Twice weekly they bake bread and every month they brew beer.

The most important of their tasks is to keep me and my apprentice supplied with yarn for our looms. My sons can help prepare the wool, but they have to be carefully watched, for cleaning the fleeces must be done properly. Faulty preparation can mean faulty yarn and with that it is impossible to make good cloth. Even more care is needed in sorting the wool, for some will make the finest worsted, while some is fit only for blankets. The spinning, at least, is light, pleasant work. During the winter the women sit by the fire in the hall, but when it is warm they take their wheels out into the sunshine.

My wife and I married for business reasons, just as my daughter will, and it has worked out very well. We have been the best of partners. If I were to die, Ann could look after the farm and the cloth making on her own. It must be understood though, that while I live, I am the master here. As St. Paul said. 'Let women be subject to their husbands and to the Lord: for the husband is the head of the woman as Christ is the head of the Church.'

Questions

1. How was an eighteenth century squire's house different from one of the sixteenth century?
2. What does the squire hope to do for each of his children?
3. What ambitions does the squire have for future generations of his family? What is he determined to avoid?
4. What people make up the clothier's family? What does he expect of each of them?

Homes and Families in the Nineteenth Century

In the nineteenth century industry grew, and so did the towns. Middle class families lived in pleasant, leafy suburbs. Their houses were built in any of the styles that had gone before, but mainly the builders were fond of copying the medieval Gothic with its pointed arches and high, pointed roofs. Though tastes had changed there were not a lot of improvements to make the homes more comfortable. Many of them now had water closets, but bathrooms were still unusual. Gas lights replaced oil lamps, but when electricity became available they were slow to use it. Central heating was almost unknown. The Victorians made a lot of progress in their industries so why did they do so little to improve their homes? Probably, the main reason was that they had servants to do all the work.

In rich and middle-class families the father had a great deal of authority. He might leave his wife to manage the servants, but his word was law. Victorian men tended to look down on women as rather beneath them. Girls were educated in the 'accomplishments' that is, they learnt skills like playing the piano, or speaking French. They were not fully educated in the sense of learning to think for themselves. A young lady might sing to a group of gentlemen, but would never dream of discussing politics with them. To the wealthy Victorian father it was unthinkable that his wife or daughter should work to earn money. That would suggest he was unable to provide for his family.

The growth of industry brought important changes for working class people. They were crowded together and many of them lived in slums, usually near the city centres. Bricks could now be mass-produced, so houses were cheap and easy to build, but apart from that, there were few technical changes. It was unusual to have drains or running water, for example.

In many trades, and during the early part of the century, it was still possible for the father and his sons to work at home. Usually, though, the women could earn more money in the factories: but they had to work very long hours. A man and his wife were no longer business partners, but spent most of their lives apart. It was impossible for these women to be good housewives. They simply did not have the time when they were grown up.

A Victorian middle-class house; much larger than most modern houses.

A barrister's daughter

My name is Emilia. Papa is a clever lawyer and a Queen's Counsel, so he is a wealthy man. We live in an elegant house, which papa has named Albert Villa. He is a great admirer of the Prince Consort. (Prince Albert, the husband of Queen Victoria). On the ground floor we have a large dining room, two even larger drawing rooms, a sewing room, a library, which also serves as a study for papa, and a schoolroom. Upstairs there are eight bedrooms, including the nursery. The kitchens are in the basement, and the servants' rooms are in the attics.

We have eight servants altogether. There is the housekeeper, who has two housemaids to help her; there is the cook and her kitchenmaid; there is also a footman, and papa is very proud to have him. It is always the mark of a good family to employ a manservant. Speaking for myself, I do not like him.

Can you guess which servant did which job in this group? Whose children do you think they are?

Emilia could be the young lady on the left, with the bored look on her face!

He is rude to the other servants, he is sometimes insolent to my friends when they call, and he eats too much. Finally, there is the governess who teaches my little brothers and sisters, and the nurse who looks after them. The servants give mama a lot of trouble. Last year she had to discharge our cook for being dirty and inefficient, and one of our housemaids has just been given warning. It seems she is to be married, but we did not even know she had a follower. Often I feel sorry for the servants, especially the kitchenmaid who has so much hard work to do, down there in the semi-darkness. But I suppose that if God had meant her to have an easy life he would not have made her a servant.

I will now describe my day to you. At about 8 o'clock one of the housemaids comes into my bedroom. She draws the curtains, lights the fire and places my bath in front of it. She then fills the bath with two cans of cold water and one of hot. At this point I am glad I am not a young man, for my brothers have cold baths, even in winter. When I have had my bath I dress myself, but when I am married, I shall expect to have a maid to help me, as mama does now.

Breakfast is at nine o'clock. We have a choice of tea or coffee with toast, fancy bread, muffins and boiled eggs.

After breakfast I may join my grown-up sister and some friends to make up a party for croquet, or archery on the lawn. Sometimes I go to the sewing room, though I have little patience for fine needlework. My sister adores it. As a child she was always making things like 'tidies' for papa's shaving paper. Now she will embroider such beautiful objects as silk fire screens. I would rather write letters, and usually find an excuse to send at least one every day. I am well pleased with a new invention called blotting paper, but I don't like the little paper bags they call 'envelopes'. I prefer to fold my letter in the shape that pleases me, and seal it with a wafer.

Lunch is a cold collation. It is not an important meal, and we do not linger over it. In the afternoons I go with mama when she takes her carriage exercise and makes her calls. She will go to a

The cover of a Victorian scrap-book.

number of houses, leaving her card if the lady is out. Usually, one of her friends will be 'at home', and we will take tea with her. Afternoon tea is now very fashionable, though some of the older people continue to offer cakes and wine.

On returning home, I go to my room where the maid brings me warm water. I wash and change for dinner. Dinner is the most important time in the day. Yesterday we had soup, turbot with lobster sauce, a leg of mutton roasted, and a charlotte of apples with apricots. It will be even more elaborate this evening as papa is entertaining important guests. Mama was discussing the menu with cook for a full hour.

After dinner we go the drawing room. Here papa may read to us, or I may sing duets with my brother while my sister plays the piano. If she wishes to sew, then I will play cards or arrange pressed flowers in my album. At eleven o'clock it is time to go to bed, though my sisters and I are usually together for half an hour or so while we brush our hair and talk about the events of the day.

I have little reason to complain for I lead a life of ease. I sometimes feel, however, that papa looks on his womenfolk as ornaments in his house, to be shown off to his friends just like his china and his paintings. When I read about the work Miss Nightingale has done in the Crimea, I wish that I, too, could be something more than a doll in a beautiful doll's house.

A visit to the family of a Wolverhampton locksmith

The town is a rabbit warren of little streets, courts and alleyways. None of them have official names, so the people have given them some well chosen names of their own, like the Pudding Bag, and Hellhouse Yard. All are piled high with cinders and refuse from the houses, so the smell is unbearable in summer.

The house I visited was in a court so narrow that the handle of the water pump was in danger of breaking a window on one side, while it must surely have flooded the house opposite if the door had been open. The house itself is three storeys high. The topmost one looks very unsafe, for the walls are cracked, and seem likely to crumble at any moment. On each floor, there is but one room, with an open flight of stairs joining them. As the house is part of a row and built back to back with yet another row, only one wall can have windows. The walls themselves are just one brick thick and are black with damp. The floor is also brick, so it too is damp and cold. The roof leaks and the windows fit badly. In winter the house is bitterly cold and in summer hot and airless. It is always dark.

Of course there is no underground drainage and all the families in the court share the one privy.

The occupant is a master lock maker. His workshop is just a lean-to shed. He works there with his two sons and a journey-man. Each one has what is called a 'standing'. This is well named, for there is no room to do anything in it but stand. The floor is of earth, and the window is just a hole in the wall. The place must be dreadfully cold in winter. Their work is little more than filing pieces of metal to shape. There is some skill in it, but none the less it is very boring. Children start the work as soon as they can hold a file. The two that I saw were aged eight and ten. The younger one stood on a block so as to reach the vice.

The man made a pretty fair lock, he told me, but trade was bad. There was much competition between the lockmakers in the town, and the factors took advantage of this. They paid little more for the locks than the value of the iron in them. He got

A Victorian slum.

Homes and Families

A locksmith at work.

A street market, 1872.

is dark. They light their stalls with candles, putting their best joints to the front and keeping the rest back in the dark. Cows, calves, sheep and pigs that die whether it is by accident or disease, are bought by the butchers. They made no secret of the fact, nor do the people object to eating meat from an animal that has died of disease. Much bad fish is also sold. The small employers give it to their apprentices who are often ill as a result.

1/9d a dozen for his padlocks. I have seen others just like them on sale in London at a shilling each. The most that man could earn in a week was ten shillings.

The lockmaker's wife, like so many in this town, worked in a factory. She had learnt nothing about the care and management of a home. She could not sew, she could not cook anything but the simplest of dishes, and she did not have enough arithmetic to add up a bill. She had great difficulty in spending the small sum of money her husband gave her at all wisely. It seems the family ate quite well at the beginning of the week, but then starved towards the end. I noticed that instead of slicing her bread neatly she cut it in chunks, and some of it was wasted. This poor woman had to work many long hours in a nearby factory, making iron nails and tips for heavy boots. It is small wonder she had little energy or time left to clean her house and care for her family.

When I visited the market I saw something of the food that is provided for the poor of Wolverhampton. Large quantities of bad meat are sold, especially veal. Most of this comes from the country butchers who wait outside the town until it

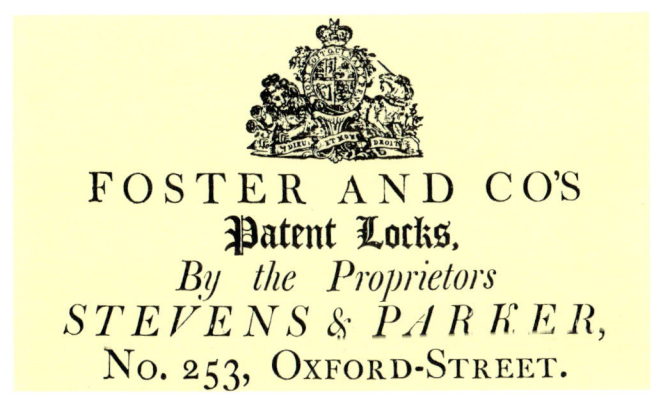

A lockmaker's sign. Do you think that Stevens and Parker is a larger firm than the one described? Why?

Questions

1 Draw a plan of the barrister's house.
2 What servants does he have? What work do they do?
3 How do the wife and daughter of the barrister spend their day? How does the daughter feel about her life?
4 Draw a plan of a street in Wolverhampton, and one of a locksmith's workshop.
5 How do the locksmith, his wife and children spend their day? Why are their lives unpleasant?
6 Contrast the food of rich and poor.

Homes and Families in the Twentieth Century

By the middle of the nineteenth century the towns had grown rapidly. Millions of people were living in houses quite as bad as the one at Wolverhampton, which you read about in the last section. One reason was that no-one had any control over the builders, who put up houses just as they pleased, only caring to make them as cheap as possible.

Then, in 1874, Benjamin Disraeli became Prime Minister. His government gave local authorities the power to pull down slums and build new houses in their place. Some towns like Birmingham, made big improvements, but over the country as a whole, not enough was done. The population grew faster than the number of houses. In the 1890s there were still some one-room houses, each with nine or more occupants.

During the early years of the twentieth century there were new forms of public transport—electric trams, motor buses, and in London, the underground railway. What followed was rather like the bursting of a dam. People who had needed to live within walking distance of their place of work found they could travel quite easily. They flooded out of the city centres, and the towns spread far and wide. There was so much 'ribbon development' along the main roads that the government had to stop it to preserve the countryside. Instead, builders had to make compact estates, with new roads.

Many families, though, were too poor to move and there were still parts of the big cities where most of the houses were slums, and where there was still bad overcrowding. One such area was the East End of London. After the Second World War, local authorities made determined efforts to solve this problem. The next two sections will show you what happened.

A member of the London County Council, 1945

The East End of London is a national disgrace. Nearly all the houses are more than a hundred years old, and they were badly built in the first place. Some people have gone so far as to say that Hitler did us a good turn by destroying many of these slums with his air raids. In fact, the air raids have been a disaster in every way. For each house

Many people in London lived on in houses almost as badly damaged by bombs as this.

destroyed, a hundred have been shaken by the explosions. Their roofs leak, their walls are cracked and their chimneys are tottering, ready to fall. Added to that, there are not nearly enough houses. In the 1930s there were three families to every two dwellings. Because so many women and children have been evacuated the population has fallen temporarily. Germany will soon be defeated, though, and all these folk will come streaming back and the overcrowding will be worse than it has ever been.

From the simple fact that houses are poor, all sorts of evils have followed. Obviously there has been overcrowding. A young couple marry, they can find no home of their own so they have to live either with the wife's parents, or the husband's. Soon they have a baby or two, and then their troubles really begin. The best they can hope for is two upstairs rooms so tiny that, as I have heard

Homes and Families

This 1951 family was forced to live in a single room, 3m × 2m

some of them say, 'When one of us breathes in, the other must breathe out'. There will be one lavatory they all share with four or five other families. There is no bathroom, of course, so every drop of water has to be carried up as many as three flights of stairs. If the baby has a bath, which is not often, it will be in a tub filled from kettles.

Obviously there is a lot of dirt, and some people have bed bugs and body lice. That means there is disease. I know of plenty of children who have caught diphtheria from drinking contaminated water.

Husbands have no share in the life of the home. A man will not do the washing up, or take the baby for a walk. Even worse, he may ill-treat his wife and

Down the local. A pleasant, but expensive, alternative to a crowded house for many men.

children. I don't agree with that, of course, but I can understand how it happens. A market porter, for example, works a twelve hour day, and when he staggers home at the end of it, what does he find? There is his tired, untidy, pregnant wife, there is a room full of children, some shouting, some crying, some quarrelling, there is a pitiful little fire burning in the grate, almost hidden by a pile of damp washing. A plate of poor, badly cooked food is thrust in front of him, and when he has eaten it, he immediately goes out to the pub. That will be the only place he can find warmth, comfort and good company. Drink is a great problem here. It helps a man forget his cares for a time, but he spends money badly needed for food and clothing. In the end it leaves him bad tempered, so his wife and children suffer.

It is not only the men who make trouble. The women are on top of each other in their wretched little houses so they are bound to fight. I do not see how three generations can live together happily. The young mother will have her own ideas on how to look after children, and the grandmother will have hers. Also, the mother knows she must discipline her children, if they are to grow up properly. The grandmother will not feel this need, and will want to spoil them. That is one of the main reasons for family rows but there are plenty more. The young wife will have to share a kitchen with its one sink and one gas stove. It is bad enough if she is with her mother, but much worse if she is with her mother-in-law. The older woman will think she is the only one who can cook for her beloved boy, and will be very irritated when the younger woman does anything different. If a newly married couple are to have a fair start in life, they must have a house of their own. There is no other way.

After the First World War there was a lot of talk of 'houses fit for heroes to live in'. All they had were slums, soup kitchens and dole queues. Things will be different this time. There will be a new and better scheme of national insurance which will take away the dread of unemployment and there will be a national health service to remove the fear of disease. Both these things will be the work of the government. In my view, though, local authorities like the London County Council will have an even more important part to play. We will build a new Britain—literally. Since bad housing caused all the problems I have described to you, then good housing can end them. In my mind's eye I can see splendid new estates in the green fields of Essex, with contented families living in comfortable homes, and children playing in the fresh air.

A housewife on a London County Council housing estate, 1952

Bill and I got married before the war. We didn't have any children at first, but after Bill was demobbed we had three in five years. There are two boys, Gary and Philip and a little girl, Linda. We couldn't live with our parents because our younger brothers and sisters were still at home. We thought ourselves lucky to have two rooms at the top of a house in the same turning as Mum's. They were damp, though, and it was impossible to keep them clean. It was no place to bring up kids, especially as they had to play in the street where I couldn't keep an eye on them.

Then the Council started moving people to estates like this. Bill and I visited one and after a lot of talking we decided to put our names on the housing list. We did it for the sake of the children. Our rooms were so bad that it wasn't long before they gave us this house.

You can see what we have. There are three good bedrooms, a nice fitted kitchen and a big living room with a slow burning stove to heat the hot water. We have an inside lavatory, of course, all to ourselves, and a bathroom. I used to hump my water up two flights of stairs, now I just turn on a tap. At the front of the house we have a flower garden and a little patch for vegetables at the back. Just half a mile away there are green fields with real cows.

When we arrived here I could hardly believe it was all real, but do you know, for the first month I hardly stopped crying! I can't say I'm happy now, even after three years.

For a start there is all the expense. The rent of this house is three times what we were paying in Poplar. Then there are Bill's train fares. There are a few factories on the estate, but they make things like car tyres and washing machines. Bill is a french polisher, so there is no work for him. He has had to keep his old job and travel daily. On top of that we needed all sorts of things for the house. We simply had to have new furniture for this smart house, and new carpets and curtains as well. We didn't have the money of course, so that meant a lot of hire purchase. We can only make ends meet because Bill has given up drinking. He used to enjoy a glass of beer on an evening, but not any more.

One problem for me is that there is nothing to do out here, and it's always so quiet that I feel I could go mad sometimes. In Poplar I was always popping out to the shops, and the streets were crowded with people. There was usually someone I knew and could have a chat with. The shops here

A post-war council housing estate.

are a mile away, so I only go a couple of times a week now. I used to go round to Mum's every afternoon too, but now I stay in the house most of the time. The boys are at school and there is only Linda. Bill leaves at seven in the morning and doesn't get home until seven in the evening. All he wants to do then is flop in an armchair and listen to the radio, and I don't blame him. I don't know what we would do without it. We would like a television one day, but they are so expensive.

Then again, people out here are so unfriendly. Back in Poplar I knew almost everyone. I had been to school with a lot of the younger ones and many of the older ones were friends of Mum's or of someone in the family. I don't know anyone here and it seems they don't want to know me. There's too much petty jealousy, that's the trouble. Bill likes gardening and he made our front look really nice. Blow me, if the people next door didn't dig up theirs and make it look exactly the same. Then she bought new curtains. I knew that made her feel good by the way she looked at ours, so I bought a new rug and hung it on the line where I knew she would be sure to see it.

The worst thing of all is that I don't see my family more than once a week. I was a little tearaway when I was young but when I was married and had kids I saw what a good friend I had in Mum. We used to do everything together, and I spent more time at her house than in my own place. Usually one of my sisters would be there and often one or other of my aunts, and we would chat away for hours. Each time I had a baby Mum was there to help. She did all the washing and cooking until I could get up. She helped me look after the babies too. I didn't trust those nurses at the clinic, but Mum brought up seven kids of her own. What she

Once in their new homes, people felt they had to buy new things, often because their friends or neighbours had them.

doesn't know about babies isn't worth knowing. When I was very tired or ill Mum always took the kids off my hands and of course my sisters were always around to help too. What would happen if I was ill out here? Bill couldn't have time off work and I would never dream of asking her next door. When I was in Poplar I had my family so I didn't need anybody else. Here I still feel like a stranger and I think I always will. I miss my old home, I miss my sisters and I miss my Mum.

Homes and Families: Conclusion

In the home there have been a great many changes and most of them for the better. Few of us can live in the style of an eighteenth century country gentleman, but we can make our houses attractive and comfortable. There have been valuable technical improvements, the most important being in plumbing and sanitation. More recently, electrical gadgets have set women free to make drastic changes in their lives. Housework can still be hard and boring, but it is nothing like the drudgery it once was.

There are still serious problems, though. Many of our houses are old and uncomfortable, or even insanitary, and parts of our cities are still overcrowded. As you have seen, many people did not like new council estates out in the suburbs. They wanted to stay where they were. The old slums had to be pulled down however, and if ordinary houses were put in their places they would be just as overcrowded. Then someone had a bright idea. If people were too thick on the ground and did not want to spread sideways, why not move them upwards? The result was the high rise blocks of flats which we now see everywhere.

Unfortunately, the high rise flats have proved as unpopular as the new council estates. Their tenants say they are inhuman; they attract vandals; if, as often happens, the lift breaks down, old people or women with prams, babies and loads of shopping have great difficulty climbing up all the flights of stairs. Life can be especially trying for a mother with young children. If she makes them stay in the flat, they do not have enough room and their noise upsets the neighbours; if she lets them go outside, she cannot keep an eye on them.

Too many of our people still cannot have the homes which they want. At present, though, the population of Britain is falling. Could this be the answer to the problem?

Questions

1 What attempts were made to improve cities in the nineteenth century? Why did they fail?
2 How did cities develop in the early twentieth century?
3 What problems might a young couple living in the East End of London have to face?
4 What was done to make the post-war estates and their houses attractive? Why might a family living there be unhappy?
5 How have houses improved over the centuries? What problems remain?

2 Leisure

Leisure in the Eighteenth Century

In the early days of fox hunting the horses were unable to jump many of the fences.

In the eighteenth century they had many of the sports which we have today, such as horse racing, hunting, shooting, boxing, cricket and football. However, they had quite different rules, and sometimes, no rules at all.

Football was often played between two villages—literally. The game began in one place and finished in the other. Anyone who wished could join in, and all the players behaved like the worst of the fans today.

Cricket was played with two stumps a foot high and placed wide apart, the space between them being known as the popping hole. A batsman was out if he failed to put his bat in the popping hole before the wicket keeper put the ball there. Bowlers threw the ball underhand, along the ground, and through rough grass, so they did not have much chance to show any skill.

Horse racing took place on any open common. There were no stands, so people could watch free of charge. Jockeys were allowed to jostle and to cross each other's paths, which meant a race was rather like a running battle. When it was over a jockey might be beaten up, either for winning or losing. If a jockey fell, any spectator could mount his horse and finish the race for him.

Guns had become more accurate, so shooting replaced hawking which had been very popular. A sportsman was still lucky if he hit his target, however, and there was always a chance that his gun might explode, blowing off his hand.

Boxing matches were fought with bare fists, and a man could have an eye knocked out or his jaw broken. Until there were rings, well above ground level, spectators sometimes joined in the fight.

Fox hunting spread slowly from the North of England, but the usual quarry was hares. People kept packs of harriers, but they did not take a lot of care in their breeding. Hunting horses, too, were not bred specially until the second half of the century. Most villages were still without enclosures, so there were fewer jumps than later on. If a huntsman did come to a hedge or fence, he usually dismounted, and helped his horse over.

As well as these sports there were others that were later forbidden, like cock fighting and bear baiting.

Generally, then, sport in the eighteenth century was unscientific, disorganized and cruel. There were people, however, who wanted to enjoy themselves in a dignified way, as you will see in the case study on Bath.

A visitor to London describes blood sports

The most popular sport is cock fighting. Fighting cocks are large, ugly birds. They are specially bred and some of them have pedigrees like dogs or, indeed, noblemen. A good bird may be worth as much as five pounds.

The stage on which they fight is quite small. First, each cock appears on his own, and struts about so that the spectators can decide which one they want to back. When the bets have been placed, the two birds are put at opposite ends of the stage. They immediately rush at each other, and fight fiercely. They wear silver spurs so they can do each other a great deal of harm.

The fight is often to the death. Sometimes one cock will be killed very quickly, but the combat can last for an hour. The birds show great courage, and unexpected things can happen. I have seen a cock exhausted, badly wounded and ready to die,

A cockfight, by the well-known artist, Hogarth

Bull baiting. What modern breed of dog do the dogs in the picture resemble?

somehow regain his vigour and go on fighting. One was actually lying on the stage and his opponent jumped on his body, crowing with triumph. The fallen bird suddenly leapt to his feet and killed his rival. Such things do not often happen, but the fact that they can, helps make the fights exciting.

The crowd is mainly of common people, and the noise they make is deafening. Gentlemen of quality attend as well, and though they may be quieter in their behaviour they place much heavier bets. It is not unknown for £500 to be won—and lost–on a single fight.

The following notice advertised other kinds of sport:

> **At the Bear Garden in Clerkenwell Green.**
>
> These are to give Notice to all gentlemen and Gamesters, that this present Monday, there will be a match fought by four Dogs at the Bull. And a bull let loose to be baited with fireworks all over him and Dogs after him.
> With other Variety of Bull Baiting and Bear Baiting, Being a general day of Sport by all the Old Gamesters.

In bull baiting, the bull is tethered by the horns, with a rope about fifteen feet long. The dogs are then let loose at him. They try to run under his belly, and seize him from below. The bull beats the ground with his feet, which he keeps as close together as possible, and he threatens the dogs with his horns. He does not try to gore his enemy, but to slide a horn beneath him and throw him. Sometimes, with a mere twist of the head, he will send a dog flying thirty feet into the air. If the dog is unlucky he will fall with a thud and that will break his back. Often, though, the spectators save him. They bend their backs to give him a soft landing, or catch him on a long pole, held slantways, so that he slides to the ground. Unless he is completely unconscious he will return to the attack.

If a dog once obtains a hold, the bull bellows with rage and pain and flings him about in all directions. But either the dog tears out the flesh he is biting, or he keeps his hold. Nor can the dog's owner make him let go by calling him, or even beating him. While a group of men hold the bull, others force a pole between the dog's jaws and prize them apart. There is no other way.

As a change from watching animals die, it is often possible to witness a hanging. As many as a dozen criminals may be executed at a time, and it is quite a spectacle.

The condemned prisoners, wearing white shirts

A public execution

and caps, are carried in carts to Tyburn, which is half a mile outside the city. Some are quite unconcerned, while others who are full of drink, mock and jeer at the crowd. At their destination they are put on a specially wide cart, and each criminal has a noose round his neck. A chaplain on the cart makes the condemned men pray and sing a few verses of the psalms. Relatives can mount the cart to say farewell. After about a quarter of an hour the cart is drawn away and the criminals are left hanging. Sometimes, friends and relations tug at their feet so that they may die more quickly. After the execution there are often fights between parents and others who want to take the bodies for burial and messengers sent by surgeons who want the bodies for dissection.

There are stands near the gallows so that spectators can have a good view. There is always a large crowd which enjoys itself hugely.

Richard Nash of Bath

My name is Richard Nash, though because of my fondness for fine clothes, I am known as 'Beau' Nash. My father, a respectable glass manufacturer of Swansea, was ambitious for me. He sent me first to Oxford, and then bought me a commission in the Guards. I had no liking for the rough life of a soldier, and wished rather to follow that of a gentleman of leisure. Here, I fear, I met a problem. A gentleman needs the rents from many broad acres if he is to live in style and what chance had I of acquiring an estate? I had but one asset. When I was at Oxford I became skilful at cards, so I could make quite a good living from gambling.

I first came to Bath in 1705 and saw at once that there were possibilities. It is an old Roman city, but more important than that, it has hot springs whose waters can work cures that are nothing short of miraculous. From hard drinking and hard living the members of our aristocracy contracted gout and many other ailments, so they came here in large numbers. Between taking their cures, they indulged themselves in their favourite pastime of gambling. I joined them at the card tables and won enough from them to live in comfort.

In those days Bath was in disorder. The houses were old and inconvenient, the streets narrow and full of filth, while the only building with any dignity was the Abbey. The behaviour of the visitors matched the buildings. Their manners were a disgrace. It was not unusual to see gentlemen come to a ball, wearing boots and swords. They were, however, sensitive on points of honour and duels were common. Public events, such as there were, lacked any organization.

To try to keep some sort of order, the Corporation had appointed a Master of Ceremonies, Captain Webster. Instead of preventing disputes, he involved himself in them and it was not long before he was killed in a duel. That was my opportunity, for I took his place as Master of Ceremonies. I set an example in my own dress and behaviour, and drew up a strict code of rules. I made it plain that I expected everyone to obey them to the letter, and most people welcomed my authority. I now ensure that Bath society is the most elegant and best conducted in England. Just once in a while someone presumes to defy me, but I am impressed by neither rank nor title. As I once told a princess, 'I reign here and my laws must be kept'. At Bath there is a quaint habit of electing the most worthy citizen 'King of Bath'. It was not long before I had that honour.

One of my first concerns was to give our visitors dignified surroundings. There was a time when onlookers pelted patients bathing in the hot waters

'Beau' Nash.

Leisure

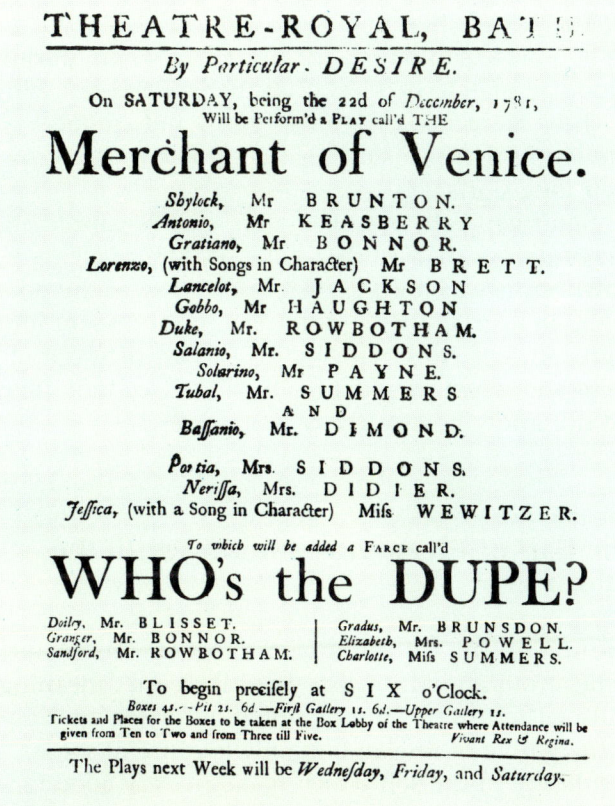

Royal Crescent, Bath.

A 'double-bill' at the Theatre Royal, Bath (top) and a masquerade (above).

with dead rats. Now we have the King's Bath which is quite enclosed, where sufferers can bathe in peace. Beside it is the Pump Room. From eight in the morning this is crowded with people, anxious to drink the healing waters. Music is played to divert them. There is an Assembly Room and a Ball Room which are very spacious and appear most striking, particularly at night when they are lit up. People gather here during the day to chat, drink tea and play cards. Twice weekly there is a ball. There are two theatres, which offer plays for people of refinement and good taste. Bath also has a number of excellent bookshops. Here, for a subscription of as little as £2 a year you may read novels, plays and newspapers, as well as reports on what is happening in Bath. If you add to all this the coffee houses and the numerous splendid shops, you will see that our visitors lack nothing for their entertainment.

I am happy to say that the quality of the buildings is beginning to match the quality of the life here. Mr. Ralph Allen has some quarries on Combe Down which yield the most excellent stone. He has an ingenious railway, worked by gravity, to carry it from the top of the hill. There is also an architect, John Wood, who is putting this stone to the best possible use by building elegant houses in the classical style. He has just finished Queen's Square, which is the envy of other cities. His son, also called John, has ambitious plans for the whole of the town. They include a magnificent crescent of houses on the slopes of Lansdowne Hill.

The people of Bath should be grateful to Ralph Allen, the two John Woods, and of course, to me. Between us we shall make this city even more splendid than it was in Roman times.

Questions

1 List the eighteenth century sports which we still have today. How have they changed?
2 What were the main blood sports of the eighteenth century?
3 Why was Bath a popular place in the eighteenth century? How was it changed into a pleasant city?
4 Contrast the pleasures of Bath with those of watching blood sports. Did the same people enjoy both, do you think?

Leisure in the Nineteenth Century

In the nineteenth century the worst of the old blood sports were stopped. For example, Parliament made bear baiting illegal in 1835 and cock fighting in 1849. There were no more public hangings after 1868.

Sports became much more civilized. Quite a number of public schools were founded and their headmasters felt that organized games would develop the characters of their boys. That could only happen, of course, if the games were played in an orderly way. As a result, very strict rules were drawn up and it became the mark of a 'good sportsman' to obey them. Soon, other people than public school boys were playing their games in the same spirit.

Football became very much as it is today. Boxers wore gloves, so they could not damage each other badly, and neither could a man pick up his opponent by the hair with one hand, and hit him with the other.

Games grew more scientific. The invention of the lawnmower in the 1830s meant cricketers could play with more skill. Overarm bowling was made legal after 1864, and batsmen improved too. In the eighteenth century it was a good team that made a hundred runs, but by the end of the nineteenth century W. G. Grace was scoring centuries on his own. On the hunting field the careful breeding of horses made the sport faster and more exciting.

Some games gained in popularity. Cricket spread from the south of England to the north. Football was the national sport by the end of the century.

There were new games, as well. In 1823 William Webb Ellis began one at Rugby school when, during a football match, he picked up the ball and ran with it. There were also golf, lawn tennis and croquet. The last of these was especially suitable for ladies in their long skirts.

Sport generally was becoming well organized and less brutal, so that it was a good deal more pleasant. However, it was not for everyone. Many of the poor in the industrial towns lived in slums and spent long hours at their work. Their spirit was crushed out of them and when they did have a little free time they did not know how to enjoy themselves.

The Earl of Plymouth—hunting with the Quorn

I hunt with the Quorn in Leicestershire. (The name comes from an old English word 'Cweorn', meaning 'Mill'.) There is no county equal to this for hunting in the whole of England, mainly because of some peculiarity in the soil which makes it very good for scent. Once the hounds have the scent of a fox it is most unusual for them to lose it. Also, this is grazing country, with grass fields that are almost like velvet. It is impossible to ride fast over arable, so the hunting is never so good in counties where the farmers plough most of their land. Moreover, Leicestershire has plenty of furze breaks where the foxes have their earths, but in contrast there are few large woods where they may escape from the hunt.

Here, as elsewhere there have been many Enclosure Acts, so there are numerous hedgerows. Most of them are 'bullfinch fences' which are blackthorn hedges with a ditch on one side. Some of them are so high that a horse cannot clear them, but he may jump through the topmost branches. More formidable is the ox-fence which is a wide ditch, a dense hedge of blackthorn and then, two yards beyond that, a four foot high wooden fence. Only the best of horses can clear it, and to do so puts a great strain on them. There are some who claim these hedgerows ruin the hunting, but a man of spirit will say they are a challenge to his skill and add excitement to the chase.

I keep twenty-four hunters altogether. That may seem a great many; after all, I can only ride one at a time. I would agree that I have plenty and most of my friends make do with ten. You must remember, though, that the pace of the hunt is much faster than it was. I have to change my hunter at least

Rugby school, showing an early version of the game in progress.

once, as to ride him to the end of the day would be to ride him to his death. Also a horse needs five days rest after a moderate run, and seven or even eight after a severe one. Moreover, one horse in six is usually lame, or unfit for some other reason. You will understand then, that if a man wishes to hunt six days in the week, ten or a dozen horses is the minimum he must have.

Hunting is expensive. A good horse is worth over two hundred pounds, and to maintain my stud of twenty-four at Melton Mowbray costs me two thousand pounds a year. There is no other way, I assure you, in which I would choose to spend my money.

It is a pleasure to dress in style. The Meltonian fox-hunter is the most distinguished of his kind. His coat and breeches fit exactly, the leather of his boots shines, and his horse is groomed to perfection. His whole air is one of quality and high breeding. Far more important though, is the excitement of the chase.

Picture to yourself a green field, perhaps of a hundred acres. First come the hounds in a body, racing so fast that they have little time for baying. Just now and then one will give tongue as if to remind his friends that the villain fox is just ahead. The sound is music to the ears of the huntsmen. Close behind the pack come the best of the riders, but never so close that they ride into it. Nothing angers me more than to see a clumsy oaf do this and injure a hound so that it has to be destroyed. The leaders go as straight as the hounds, and as fast, clearing the hedgerows as lightly and as magically as if they were dropping from heaven. The less skilful, and the unlucky, soon trail behind. Two riderless horses are seen in the distance, and the story is that someone has broken an arm. The going, though, is too good to enquire further. Away to the left there is a crashing sound. A horse in trying to clear some rails has landed on them instead, and flung his rider into the ditch. The going, though, is too good for anyone to stop and give help. One thing matters, and one thing only, and that is to chase the villain fox to his death.

A 'folk' painting of a fox hunt. These nineteenth-century horses are clearing the fences with ease (see p. 16).

Leisure

Hunting is much improved, being faster than it ever was. Hounds were always bred for scent, but now they are bred for speed as well. To keep up with them, faster horses were needed, and this, too, has been achieved. Breeding is now a scientific process, and there has been so much success with horses and hounds that livestock farmers are now using the same methods.

A visit to the locksmiths of Wolverhampton

The lockmakers of Wolverhampton are most foolish in their working habits. They carry on their trade in their own workshops, so they can please themselves what hours they keep. None of them does anything on Monday, and most of them idle away Tuesday as well. On Wednesday they start in earnest but they do not exert themselves, so on Thursday and Friday they have to work themselves and their families almost to death. On Saturday morning they rise at 5.00 a.m. and by ferocious efforts finish all they are supposed to do.

At about two o'clock those that did some work on Tuesday leave their houses: masses more join them at four or five o'clock: by seven o'clock the streets, the market, the beer shops and the gin shops are full of people.

As Saturday is pay day, the market is crowded like a fair, and so are the streets leading to it. Among the crowds milling up and down you will often find a group standing still. Some form a ring round a pair of coal miners who are dancing. Often they dance to the sound of a fiddle, but failing that, they make their own music by singing. Another group may be listening to a ballad singer, and another to some fellow who has just seen the latest executions outside Stafford gaol. A seller of quack medicines will always draw a crowd with tales of his wonderful cures for coughs, colds and broken limbs.

Meanwhile a deafening noise of singing and

A Sunday morning street scene.

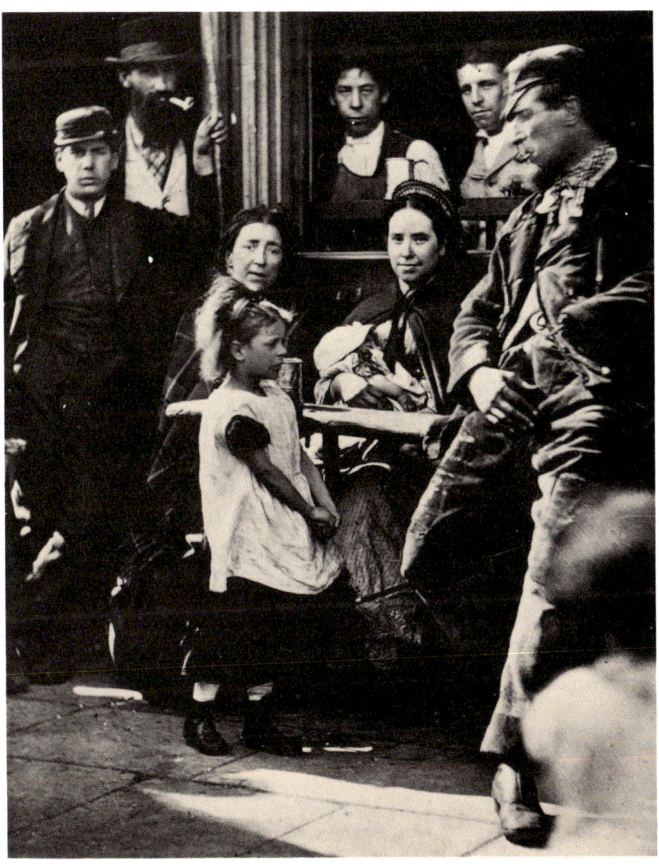

Outside a beer house.

shouting is coming from the beer houses. The doorways and passageways to them are packed with customers, while the serving girls are struggling to bring them their drink without pouring it over them or dropping the mugs. All the noise and capering come from the miners. You will sometimes see one leaping about, his short pipe stuck in his mouth, his arms extended with a jug in one hand, a glass in the other and the beer going everywhere. The lockmaker sits quietly with his long pipe, and holds his glass carefully, as with a grave look, he drinks it to the bottom.

Towards midnight there are often quarrels and fights.

On Sunday morning the adults are dead and listless. The women, in their working dresses stand about at their doorways. They are dirty and so are their homes. Some of the houses do indeed have their brick floors washed and sanded, but their owners are selling things like cakes, oranges and sugar sticks. The cleaning is done to attract customers.

The men wander about a bit, some on their own and some in groups. They wear their working aprons and caps, their faces are dirty and unshaven and their grubby sleeves are rolled up to reveal arms stained with soot. Many have been working all night to make up for their idleness in the week. Others are recovering from their heavy drinking of the evening before. A man will lean against a wall, smoking and watching the people go by, but paying no real attention to them. I once saw a group of five, still and silent, leaning on the wall of a pig sty staring at the pigs. The pigs were staring back at them, their snouts pointing up to the men's faces, and wondering what would happen. Nothing did.

Only the children show any signs of life. There are groups sitting on dirt heaps, chirping like sparrows, and all of them much the same colour. Others are chasing about on a piece of waste ground behind the church. Some little boys have a small pick-axe and they are sitting in a hole, pretending to be miners. Lads of about fifteen are playing with marbles. Two boys are fighting, both are swearing, and one has a bleeding nose. In one of the courts six girls, aged from nine to fifteen are jumping from the piles of dung and rubbish. Every so often one of them sprawls on the ground, but is soon on her feet again, scuttling up the nearest dirt heap.

There are no men out walking with their wives. Everyone seems dead and indifferent. There is no laughter, there are not even any smiles. Only the girls playing on the dirt heaps are showing any high spirits.

Questions

1 What changes were made in sport in the nineteenth century?
2 Why is Leicestershire a good country for hunting?
3 What were the attractions of fox hunting? How has the sport changed since the eighteenth century?
4 How did the people of Wolverhampton spend a) their working week b) Saturday night? How did this affect the way they spent Sunday?
5 How did the children enjoy themselves?
6 Why were there such big differences between the pleasures of men like the Earl of Plymouth and those of the locksmiths?

Leisure in the Twentieth Century

Leisure is much more important today than it has ever been. For one thing, people have more spare time. The working week is five days instead of six and holidays are much longer than in the past. Also religion is not as important as it was, so no-one is in disgrace if he plays games on Sunday.

Moreover, our whole attitude to work has changed. In Victorian times serious people put their work first. They only took leisure so that they could come back to their work refreshed, and be better at it. Today, we tend to put our leisure first and only go to work so that we can earn the money to pay for it. None the less, our work does have a big influence on how we enjoy ourselves.

If a man has low wages he obviously cannot afford a yacht, while someone with a well-paid job has a much wider choice of things to do. There is more to it than that, though. It is possible to have one of three attitudes towards your work. You may enjoy it, you may dislike it, or you may not care very much one way or the other. If someone enjoys his work he will probably do something like it in his spare time. An electronics engineer, for example, might fix up gadgets in his home, or a mechanic might build go-karts. If someone hates his work he will do something quite different. Many coal miners keep racing pigeons. What both of these groups have in common is that they want to do something for themselves.

Others, simply feel their work is 'all right' and put up with it. They are neither attracted to something like it, nor driven to something quite different. As they are not too bothered about their work, they are not too bothered about their leisure. They just want to sit back and be entertained.

The third group is by far the largest, so a great many leisure industries have grown up to keep it amused. There are radio, television, the cinema, package holidays and many more. The case study is of a holiday camp. These became especially popular after the Second World War, but are now in competition with cheap holidays abroad, particularly to Spain.

In the 1950s more people found they were able to afford a seaside holiday. Advertisements like these tried to lure them to different holiday camps.

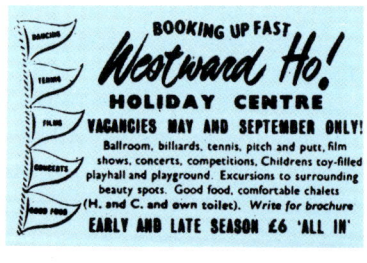

'Happy campers' having fun. One feature of early holiday camps was the organised activities.

A manager of a holiday camp in the 1950s

I am the manager of a large holiday camp on the south coast. I suppose you could say that my job is to sell pleasure. Pleasure, though, is a very difficult thing to sell. If it's bread, you can get the weight of your loaf right, as well as its taste and its shape. Your customer knows just what he is buying. Even with a complicated article like a motor car there are plenty of things to go on, like the size of engine, miles per gallon, acceleration and so forth. We can only hope our campers go away feeling they have had value for money, or else they won't come back again.

In fact, lots of them do return, I'm pleased to say. They come back year after year, so we must be giving them the kind of holiday they enjoy.

One of my main problems is my staff. I have an assistant and a secretary who are both very reliable and an excellent entertainment manager. There are other people with quite important responsibilities such as those in charge of the chalets, the cafe, the shop, the nursery and security. We also need a large number of helpers like porters, cooks, waiters and waitresses, shop assistants and 'uncles' and 'aunties' to look after the small children. Only a nucleus of us are permanent, because the camp is closed for much of the year. The best workers have regular employment so they don't want to work for us. We have to take what people we can find. Usually they are quite young, and have changed jobs so often that they have no problem in getting on with strangers. This is good of course, but they have no sense of loyalty. They work here to make as much as they can and will leave at the drop of a hat for any reason you care to mention. I am supposed to dismiss anyone who is violent or drunk, but I can't do that at the height of the season. They know this and behave as they please. The kitchen staff steal food, barmen help themselves to drink, and waiters will take any tip that is offered, however large. Quite often those that are off duty in the evening crowd the bar so that it is almost impossible for the campers to buy a drink. On the other hand, some staff can be over sensitive. For example, if a waitress has an argument with a rude camper at breakfast, she can be in a bad mood and not speak a civil word for the rest of the day. Everyone who works here despises the campers and it sometimes shows. This is a pity, because most campers want the staff to like them, even if it is only in the hope of getting favours, like extra helpings at mealtimes.

What makes people come here? I think it's mainly because life in a holiday camp is quite different from life in the outside world. That's something most of them want to forget. The man leaves his work behind as well as the living room he doesn't want to decorate. The woman has no shopping to do, no cooking and no housework. Also we separate the age groups so that adults, teenagers and small children all go their different ways and enjoy themselves as they please. Mum and Dad can forget about the kids. 'Uncles' and 'aunties' look after the little ones by day and patrol the chalets by night in case a baby starts crying. For some married people it is the only time in the year when they can be together on their own. There's an old couple who come here summer after summer. The man told me that he was a nightwatchman and hardly saw his wife except on holiday. Coming here to stay is like a second honeymoon for them. Another thing of course is that all the entertainment is free. People know exactly how much their holiday is going to cost them. They don't have to spend a lot of money on extras. The dances and the variety shows are always packed.

I'm afraid that many of the youngsters are just looking for casual affairs. They are away from home and don't have to obey any of the usual rules. They quickly find partners, and perhaps change them twice or three times in a week. Usually they give each other false names and addresses.

The pigeon fancier

I am a miner, and like lots of my mates, I keep racing pigeons. Why miners should like pigeons, I don't know, but wherever there are coal mines, there are pigeons. I suppose it might be to do with the job. Mining is hard, unpleasant, dirty and dangerous. We earn good wages, but people still look down on us. They seem to think that because we work underground we are somehow inferior, perhaps not proper human beings at all. My pigeons help me forget all that. What's more, as a breeder and trainer, I have made a name for myself, which I could never have done in my work.

Looking after pigeons takes all sorts of skills. You have to build your loft for a start, which means you have to be something of a carpenter. I am very proud of mine. It's a good solid job and will last for many years. Then there is breeding, which is a science in itself. I have several books on it, but in the end only experience will tell you which birds you should mate. I keep careful records, of course. My pigeons have pedigrees, some of them going back generations, just like racehorses. I also take note of how well each one does in its races. I have to be something of a vet, too. I care for the babies when they are injured. There are plenty of people who make a good living at any one of these three jobs, but I do all of them pretty well.

I really enjoy being in my loft. It is quiet, I am all alone and I am completely my own boss. I also have all sorts of interesting problems to solve, on breeding, feeding and training. The birds are good company too—much better than many humans. They are full of life for one thing, friendly and very loyal. I send them hundreds of miles away, yet they come home faithfully to me. I can tell you it's very exciting at the end of the race. I watch the sky anxiously, and it's a great moment when the birds come fluttering into the loft, exhausted, but safe home again. If any don't return on the Sunday, I can't go to work on Monday. I stay at home in case they come back injured.

It always amazes me that any creature as beautiful and delicate as a pigeon can have so much strength and courage. They will fly at 40 m.p.h. as long as the wind isn't against them. Our club sends them as far as Barcelona, which is about 800 miles away. I know plenty of so-called human beings who couldn't find their way home from there, whether it was by car, boat, train or aeroplane. A pigeon will do it though, using just its own wings and its own instinct. They all come back the same way, you know, following regular flight paths across the continent and the Channel. Then, when they reach Britain, they split up and each one makes his way to his own loft. From what I saw when my wife and I flew to Spain for our holidays, pigeons are much better organized than the airlines. Lots of people have written clever things about this homing instinct, but I'm sure they don't understand it. For me, this mystery is one of the attractions of pigeon racing.

The pigeon fancier relaxing in his loft.

Before the war I believe there was a lot of short distance racing. They only took the birds a few miles, so there had to be split second timing. A lot of betting went on, and I don't think that can have been a good thing. It means the money is more important than the sport, just like in horse racing and greyhound racing. There is big money in long distance racing, though. A champion bird can be worth £3,000. The total prize money in a big race can be £40,000, with a first prize of £1,500. I don't worry about winning money. I would far rather have a silver cup to join the others on my sideboard, or better still a shield for my club. The one thing that does bother me is the expense. Sending your birds to Spain or the north of Scotland is very costly.

Several of the popular routes racing pigeons use. Estimate the distance of the longest route shown.

All I hope is that pigeon racing does not become a rich man's sport. It's not just miners that do it, of course. More and more wealthy characters are taking it up. I expect they want to forget their business worries just as I want to forget the pit. They can afford everything they need, so it gives me a lot of pleasure when my birds beat theirs. Mind you, the rich characters I would really like to beat, and with my bare fists, are the ones that keep peregrine falcons. Hawking ought to be forbidden, along with all other blood sports.

One of the best things about pigeon racing is the club. It's all right to be on your own in the loft for a lot of the time, but you need to mix with other people as well. The club gives us a chance to do that. We all go there on Friday for the birds to be ringed, to have our clocks set and fill in our forms. A band plays in the bar, and we have a few drinks. On Saturday and Sunday we visit each other to compare the results. All my friends are pigeon fanciers. They are the only people I can talk to.

Some of the blokes have 'dodges' they think work wonders. They will give their birds things like linseed, quinine or salt. I don't agree with that. You can't beat good care, good breeding and a lot of careful training. I will admit mind you, that a bit of sulphur in the feed, just before the race, does seem to help.

If you like you can breed birds for their looks and show them. I don't do that, so some of my friends say I am not a true pigeon fancier. What I admire, though, is a good working bird, just as I admire a good working man.

Leisure: Conclusion

Over the years our leisure has become much more technical and more highly organized. In the eighteenth century, if people wanted some entertainment they set two cockerels to fight each other: if they wanted to play a game, a mob gathered and kicked a ball from one village to the next: if there was a horse race anyone could join in, on any sort of horse. Today, if we want entertainment we switch on the television. That may be simple for us, but the amount of science and skilled engineering in the set is enormous. Our football is played to strict rules, there is an elaborate system of matches, while running a team is as complicated as managing an important business. As for horse racing, only skilled professional jockeys and thoroughbred horses can take part in that.

Leisure has also become more and more important. Today machines and computers are taking over the tedious and humdrum jobs in factories and offices so it looks as if people are going to have even more free time in the future. Our fathers and grandfathers were ruled by their work: perhaps our children and grandchildren will be ruled by their leisure.

Questions

1. Why is leisure more important today than it has ever been?
2. How do people's jobs help decide the ways they enjoy themselves?
3. What were the problems of running holiday camps? Why were they popular, none the less?
4. Why is it interesting to keep racing pigeons? Why should it appeal to miners?
5. Contrast the pleasures of a holiday camp with those of keeping pigeons.

3 Education

Education in the Eighteenth Century

The medieval Grammar school at Higham Ferrers. Nearly all the pupils would have become priests.

In many parish churches, there is a room over the porch, and it is likely that this was the village school in the Middle Ages. A town might have a grammar school, and that, too, would be quite small. The one at Higham Ferrers, for example, is just like a tiny church, about half the size of a modern classroom. Also, there were the two universities of Oxford and Cambridge. All these places were for the sons of the poor, mainly to train them to become priests. The sons of nobles did not need book learning, but other skills such as fighting from horseback.

As the country prospered however, more and more men became merchants and traders. They wanted an education for their sons and were willing to pay for it. The schools found they could charge fees, and some, like Winchester and Eton became important 'public schools', taking pupils from all over the country. Even the small grammar schools were mainly for middle class pupils, and by the seventeenth century they were admitting hardly any children whose parents could not afford fees.

Then, in 1699, the Church of England founded the Society for the Promotion of Christian Knowledge (S.P.C.K.). One of its aims was to encourage people to start Charity Schools so that at least some poor children could have an education.

Here you will read about such a school in a small country town. First the clergyman of the parish explains how it is run, and then a girl pupil describes how she and her brother find it. They do not enjoy school, but they have more reason to be grateful than they will admit. Most of the children in the town cannot even read or write and will never learn. What is more, the school will help these pupils when they leave. It will pay a master craftsman to take the boy as an apprentice and it will find the girl a post as a maid servant in a good home. Without this help, both would face a lifetime of rough, unskilled labour.

A Charity School in 1750 described by the clergyman of the parish

When I became the Rector here in 1732 I saw that my first duty must be to start a Charity School. The church was barely half full on Sundays showing that too few people knew anything of the Word of God. The children of the poor were in danger of becoming heathens, or Presbyterians, which is nearly as bad. I must make my flock walk in the paths of the true religion which is, of course, the religion of the Church of England. To carry out my task I must have a school. It has been well said, 'Bring up a child the way he should go, and when he is old he will not depart from it.'

My predecessor was old, and I fear, lazy. I meant to show my people that their new Rector was different. I well remember my first sermon. The congregation settled down to sleep, as it had always done, but my first words woke it, like a trumpet blast. The clerk, slumped in his pulpit below mine, suddenly sat bolt upright: an old gentleman whose wig had fallen askew, pulled it straight: a young miss who had been eyeing a beau was so covered in confusion that she had to hide her face behind her fan. I spoke of the dangers of hell fire—the dangers to which they were exposing the poor by their neglect. They blinked, disbelievingly. I told them

'The sleeping congregation' by Hogarth.

Shortly afterwards we had a public meeting and many gentlemen attended. Close on a hundred made donations, some as little as a guinea, though Alderman Higgins gave £50. Altogether we had £250, which was enough to build a handsome school. More than that, each of these gentlemen agreed to subscribe ten shillings a year, which gives an annual income of £50. With this sum we can pay a master and a mistress to educate fifteen boys and fifteen girls.

The subscribers elected a Committee of Management. I am, of course, its Chairman. Alderman Higgins is Vice-Chairman. I regret that he is loud and coarse. His gout does not improve his temper, and he often has the impudence to question what I say. Still, the others do as I direct. They take it in turn to visit the school, and make sure the teachers are attending to their duties. Then they must help with the discipline of the school. I fear it sometimes happens that a child will misbehave, and the parents will be so foolish as to support the child against the teacher. When that happens I order the parents to attend before the Committee with their child. Then I reprimand them and unless they show they are truly sorry I expel the child from the school.

Another duty of the Committee is to examine children who wish to be admitted to the school. The subscribers take turns to nominate children and when any of them does so he signs a certificate to say that the parents are devout members of the Church of England, that they do not receive poor relief and are in every way deserving. They must also certify that the child will introduce no evil into the school, through bad habits or bad morals. To make sure, though, the parents and the child must appear before the Committee and only when I am satisfied is the child admitted. You may be sure that

that they faced the same dangers, and one or two looked uneasy, but not many. Then I said we must have a Charity School in the town, a school that would teach its pupils the true faith, and send them forth into the world to be honest servants and trusty apprentices. At last they were interested and though I preached for over an hour, they listened to every word.

A Dame School, where an old woman in a village would teach reading and writing. This was often the only kind of school apart from the Charity School.

we have none of the street rabble, but only worthy children of God-fearing parents.

I must explain that we in no way copy the local grammar school. That is for the sons of gentlemen who are learning to be gentlemen. Our school does not try to lift young people out of their station in life, but rather to train them to live in it. The children of servants must be servants, though never let it be thought that this is an unworthy calling. Angels themselves are ministers to God, and there was One even greater than the angels who said, 'I am among you as he that serveth'.

In spite of all the care the Committee and I give the school, we must depend much on the teachers. I am pleased to say that Mr. and Mrs. Woodward are two fine people. Mr. Woodward was a pupil at the Grammar School. His wife is not *quite* as well educated, but she has an excellent influence on the girls. You know, in the eighteen years I have been here Mr. and Mrs. Woodward have faithfully attended church twice every Sunday, and every Wednesday evening as well. Two more humble and devout people it would be impossible to find. Their Christian characters are models for the children they teach.

A Charity School girl

My brother John and I both attend the Blue School. My parents think we are very lucky to go there, but I cannot say we enjoy it. There is the uniform for a start. It is free, I know, but why can they not give us the money to buy whatever clothes we like? Blue is not a colour that suits me at all. Besides, as soon as anyone sees us they know we are at a Charity School. Mr. Snellgrove, my father's employer,

Pupils at Christ's Hospital, near Horsham, still wear old-fashioned Charity School uniforms.

nominated us and he quite often reminds me of it. 'That's a charming blue cloak you have there Jane', he will say. 'Do not forget I helped to pay for it, and so take good care of it'. Common street children mock us as well. I have had a live rat thrown at me, and John has been pelted with mud. Of course, if we do anything wrong ourselves, people know where to report us. What is worse we each have a metal badge with a number, like this one on my apron. All anyone has to do is tell Mrs. Woodward that girl number nine was being saucy, and she knows at once that it was me.

I would like the school better if I could like Mrs. Woodward. John says her husband is a strict man but fair, and he does know how to teach. Mrs. Woodward cannot teach, so we learn little from her. Also, she has her favourites, and to be one of those you have to bring her little presents and bunches of flowers. When I was quite small I called one of her favourites a liar. Mrs. Woodward took her horse-whip and she whipped me. The girl who told

the lies was not punished at all. She *was* a liar and all her family are liars. My mother wanted my father to complain, but he would not. He said that if he did the Rector would expel John and me from the school. That would have been an end to our education.

The school day is long. We start at nine in the morning and we do not leave until five in the evening in summer, though we go home at sunset during winter. On Saturday we finish at noon. We have but one hour for dinner. In the mid-morning we may have half an hour for play, if the Rector is not around. That is so that Mrs. Woodward can enjoy her pint of beer. She *is* an ignorant woman.

Lessons are dull, too. We are supposed to learn to read, to write and to reckon in the four rules. We also do needle work, and a very great deal of it. A local shop takes what we make, and the money goes to the school. I am sure Mrs. Woodward keeps much of it for herself. Once she put me alone in a small room for talking during the sewing lesson. When she let me out she said, 'You have not done much!' 'You should not have put me in here,' I answered, 'My needle goes with my tongue'. I had a good whipping for that.

One thing we hear a great deal of, is religion. We come to school twice on Sunday for an hour of Bible reading. Then we walk to church two and two, the girls behind the boys. We sit at the back of the church, and a small congregation it would be if it were not for us. The Woodwards are always preaching to us, especially about our duty to our betters.

They know all about that themselves. You should see them when the Rector visits the school. Never was there so much bowing and scraping, smiling and smarming. It is quite different as soon as the Rector leaves, of course. I once heard Mr. Woodward say, 'He has a voice like a squeaking cart wheel. How can anyone have a nap in church with a noise like that coming from the pulpit?'

Questions

1. What changes were there in the grammar schools?
2. Why did people wish to start Charity Schools? How did they do so?
3. How was a Charity School run? How were its teachers expected to behave?
4. What children were admitted to Charity Schools? What did the schools try to do for their pupils? What did they *not* attempt?
5. What subjects were taught in Charity Schools?
6. Why was life trying for a Charity School child?

Education in the Nineteenth Century

Though the Charity schools did useful work, they had very few pupils. By the early nineteenth century people were thinking that many more children should go to school. However, there was a shortage of money and teachers. To solve the problem two men, Joseph Lancaster and Andrew Bell, suggested the monitorial system. Under this a school master made his older and brighter pupils monitors. He taught them for an hour before school and they then passed on what they had learnt to the other children.

In many parishes clergy collected subscriptions to start monitorial schools, just as they had for Charity Schools. What is more, after 1833, the government began to give grants to the schools. It also started the Pupil Teacher system. Unlike a monitor, who left school at twelve or so to go into other work, a Pupil Teacher intended to make teaching his career. He worked as an apprentice in a school until he was eighteen, when he went to a Training College to finish his studies. This meant that, after a time, the country had a reasonable number of qualified teachers.

By 1860 the government had increased its grants considerably, but it also decided that the elementary schools, as they were now called, were inefficient and were not giving value for money. Therefore, in 1862, a government minister called Robert Lowe introduced a new set of regulations called the Revised Code. A school's grant now depended on how well its pupils attended and how many of them passed an examination which they sat every year in reading, writing and arithmetic. This was known as 'payment by results'.

Another problem was that many towns did not have enough schools. The churchmen who provided most of the schools tended to neglect the big cities, especially the poorer areas. To put that right there was an Education Act in 1870. It was largely the work of a government minister called W. E. Forster. Forster's Act said that if any town did not have enough schools, then its inhabitants must elect a School Board. The Board's duty was to take money from the ratepayers and use it to build the schools that were needed.

An Elementary School headmaster of 1870

Life becomes more difficult every year. Take this old building for instance. In 1830 it held some 60 boys, taught on the monitorial system, and few of them

A country schoolroom. Who is the visitor likely to be? See page 34.

An Elementary School Building

were over the age of ten. Now I have double that number, and some stay with us until they are twelve. We badly need some classrooms where my pupil teachers can take groups of the younger boys out of the way.

You will see that the floor is worn and dusty. The stove is out of order and fills the room with smoke. Even when it works it does not heat much of the room, though it roasts the boys who sit near it. Many of these windows are stuck fast, and indeed, I dare not try to open them. The wood is so rotten they would fall apart. To make things worse my scholars are not all fond of washing. Many of the parents are so afraid of their children taking cold that they sew them into thick flannel underwear at the beginning of winter, and do not remove it until the end of May. You can imagine the smell here, when to the dust and smoke are added the atmosphere from 120 boys wet through from the rain.

Discipline is a much greater problem that it used to be. I have so many more boys for one thing, and for another, I can no longer use the good old-fashioned punishments. Can you see that pulley in the roof? Many a time I have hauled a naughty boy up there in a basket. I used to tie the particularly difficult ones in sacks. Now all I can use is my cane. It is rarely idle. There are parents, though, who object even to that. A father stormed into the school the other day and threatened to knock me down if ever I touched his son again.

My teachers give me a lot of worry, too. When I became a head, all I had was a few monitors. I only needed to see them for an hour before school, to show them what to do during the day. Now, I have Pupil Teachers and I have to prepare them for their examinations. I must remain behind for two or three hours after school to instruct them in Mathematics, Geography, History, Poetry and subjects like that. It comes hard after a day struggling with the children. I suppose Pupil Teachers are a bit more help than the monitors were, because they are older. They are not much use, though, until they are eighteen, by which time their apprenticeship is over, and they leave to go to College. Some are positively unreliable. The Managers had to dismiss one last year for drinking whisky in the presence of his class.

Probably the worst thing that happened in recent years was the Revised Code. That changed the work of the inspectors completely. I never have liked inspectors, but in the old days they were not too terrible. I remember Mr. Clew used to arrive at the school late in the morning. He would see the children at work, have a quick look at the buildings, and as long as everything was in reasonable order he would write a good report. The vicar used to make doubly sure of that by giving him an excellent lunch with plenty of wine. We had no worry about the government grant in those days.

Now there is not one inspector, but two or three. They check the registers for mistakes and work out the average attendance. Then they test the boys in reading, writing and arithmetic. Every boy that attends badly and every boy that fails his examination loses the school money. The Managers have told me the school must earn a good grant or they will cut my salary. Well, you can be sure I make the boys work. Anyone that will not learn to spell, or say his tables, has a good beating as he deserves.

My latest worry is the new Education Act. I hear that the town is to have a School Board. It will build enough schools for every child and then make education compulsory. If there are brand new schools, which parents will want to send their sons to this old place? It will all be for nothing, too.

Education

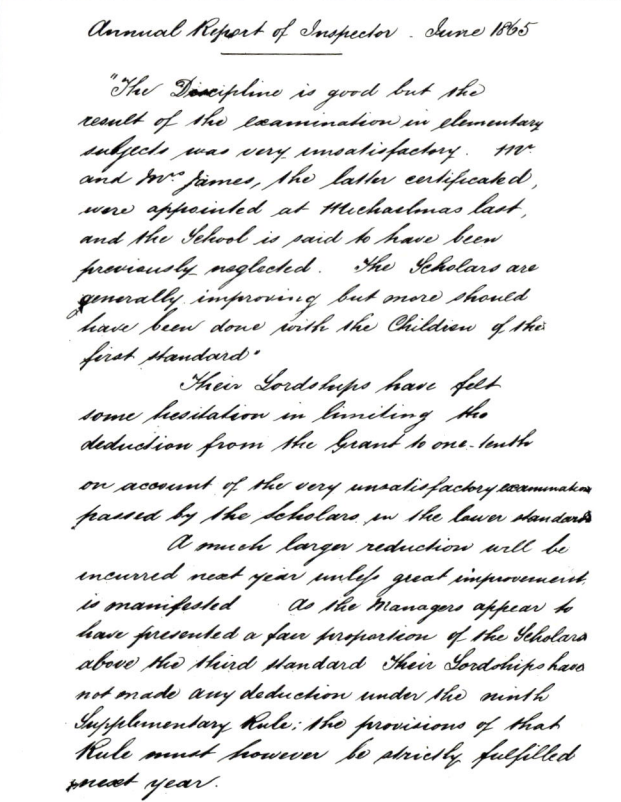

An Inspector's report

From a Victorian alphabet book.

When you have been in teaching as long as I have, you will know that there are plenty of children for whom education is a waste of time. It is hard enough to educate those whose parents want them to learn. I do not see how it would be possible to manage a school full of street urchins.

A school inspector of 1870

I became an Inspector in 1850, and since then I have seen promising changes in the schools. Perhaps the most important has been the growth of the pupil teacher system. In the old days the only help a headteacher had was from his monitors. They earned a few pence a week and had to leave as soon as they were old enough to command more. Today, every head has his apprentices, young people of fourteen and upwards. Of course they are far better teachers than the monitors were. Even more important, we now have a steady flow of qualified men and women coming into the profession. Already there are some schools which have adult assistant teachers, and I hope and pray that the time is not far off when all schools will have them.

Next, there were the changes brought by Mr. Lowe's Revised Code. I think that 'payment by results' is the popular name for the new system. Vast sums were being spent on education but I for one am quite sure the public was not having value for money. I am as devout a member of the Church of England as anyone could wish, but I must say quite frankly that many of the clergy had too narrow a view of the work of their schools. They saw them as places to teach their own faith, and little more. A school has another duty as well as the one it owes to the Church. It has a duty to the nation, and especially when it takes the taxpayers' money for its own uses. Oh yes, the schools taught religion well enough, the clergy saw to that, but the things which the nation needs were held in much less esteem.

Moreover, if a teacher can please himself, he will give his best efforts to those pupils who learn easily. The rest he will ignore, and may even persuade them to stay away from school. But the nation has need of all its citizens. Means had to be found of compelling teachers to train even the dullards to read, to write and to reckon. Ways had to be found of drawing unwilling pupils into school. All this, Mr.

Lowe's Code has done. Today, schools must earn their grants by careful, regular teaching. A thorough examination of all the children in reading, writing and arithmetic tells me how well a school has done its work, and the grant is fixed accordingly. I examine the pupil teachers, too, and make sure the head is not neglecting their education.

All this has brought a revolution in the schools. Head teachers seek out truants eagerly, while managers award prizes and certificates for good attendance. All children have a share of their teacher's attention, indeed the dull more than the bright, which is as it should be. Ample time is given to reading, writing and reckoning in the four rules, until the children master them thoroughly. Only *then* do they begin to study History, Geography, Music and the like. Certainly a child can earn grant for these subjects, but only if he has passed his examination in the 3 R's.

Now we have Mr. Forster's Act. The Churches have worked well in the cause of education, and almost every country parish has its school. Favoured areas in the towns have their schools as well, but someone must educate the street urchins of the big

A good conduct certificate from a Church School.

National Schoolmaster (going round with Government Inspector), "Wilkins, how do you bring shillings into pence?"
Pupil, "I takes it round to the Public House, sir!"

cities. If the people there continue in poverty, vice and ignorance, the future of our country will be black indeed. It amazes me that Parliament chose to give the working classes the vote before making sure they could read and write! However, this is something the School Boards will correct. The day cannot be far distant when every child in the land will be in school until the age of twelve. We shall enter a Golden Age for education.

What changes do I regret? I fear that in recent years teachers have come to dislike inspectors. Certainly we cannot come smiling into schools. We are there to probe for weaknesses, and expose failures, so that education may improve. Teachers must understand this, they must give us their trust, and must show less fear. Why, the other day when I visited an infants' school, the headmistress fainted as I walked through the door. That was quite unnecessary.

Questions

1 Describe a) the monitorial system b) the Pupil Teacher system c) the Revised Code of 1862 d) the Education Act of 1870.
2 What problems did the headmaster of 1870 have? Why did he dislike inspectors? What worries did he have about the future?
3 What changes in education was the inspector glad to see? Why? What changes did he hope to see after 1870?
4 Contrast the ideas of the headmaster with those of the inspector.

Education in the Twentieth Century

A girls' Grammar School outing in the 1960s.

By the end of the nineteenth century there were enough schools for everyone. However, all that poor children had was an elementary education, which meant they learnt reading, writing and arithmetic, but little else.

By the 1890s other countries, like the United States and Germany, were leaving Britain behind. One reason was that they were giving their children a better education, so the British government decided that this country must have secondary schools. The problem was to find someone who could build and look after them. Since 1870 there had been School Boards, but they only existed in places where there were no church schools. Also, many of them were small, being responsible for no more than a village. School Boards could not organize secondary education.

To solve the problem, in 1902 Parliament passed an Education Act abolishing School boards, and giving their schools to the County Councils. The County Councils also had the task of building secondary schools.

The new secondary schools charged fees, but soon there was a 'special place' scheme. At the age of 11 children in the elementary schools sat a difficult scholarship examination and the lucky few who passed went to secondary schools free of charge. Most failed, and stayed in the elementary schools until they were 14, when they left to start work.

In 1944 there was another Education Act. The government had decided it was unfair that some children should have a secondary education, while others did not. The Act turned many of the Elementary Schools into Primary Schools for children up to the age of 11. After that they all went to secondary schools. In most areas these were of two kinds—Grammar Schools and Secondary Modern Schools. These Grammar Schools were not the very old ones that had existed since the Middle Ages. They were the Secondary Schools that had been set up by the Act of 1902, but now had another name. The Secondary Modern Schools were former Elementary Schools adapted for older pupils. Only children who passed an examination could go to a Grammar School. Was it right to divide children in this way? After a time many people thought it was not, so County Councils introduced Comprehensive Schools, which children of all abilities could attend. Some Comprehensive Schools were brand new. Others were made by joining a Grammar School with one or more Secondary Schools. This nearly always caused problems. The case studies give the views of two teachers whose schools are to be combined in this way. One is an elderly French mistress in a Grammar School, and the other is a young woodwork master in a Modern School.

A Grammar School French mistress, 1969

I have taught at our small country grammar school for many years, and am pleased with my job because I feel I am good at it. Our children are clever and they follow an academic education with subjects such as French, German, Latin, Physics, Chemistry and English Literature. Many of our pupils go on to Universities, and we have an Honours Board showing the names of those who have done well there. Even pupils who do not go on to Universities pass their examinations well enough to find good jobs, as for example, in banking and the Civil Service.

I have no problem in deciding what to teach, because I just keep to the syllabus laid down by the Examination Board. Also, the school year follows a regular pattern. At the end of each term we give our classes revision, set them examinations and write reports: there are 'mock' public examinations in January and real ones in the Summer: we have a Speech Day in the Autumn, and a Carol Concert at Christmas. Everyone knows exactly what to do, and the whole school runs smoothly.

Now we have to change, for our local authority

has decided to turn its Grammar and Secondary Modern Schools into Comprehensive Schools. We are dismayed to find we must amalgamate with a secondary school twice our size, and in buildings a mile away. You can imagine the problems this will cause. How is it possible to have one school in two buildings, and such different buildings at that? For example, we have laboratories for Advanced Science and an excellent library, while they have plenty of workshops and domestic science rooms. We think it would be best to keep the more able children in our building, and send the remainder to the other.

The parents of our pupils are worried about how the new system will change our school. Most of them cannot bear the thought of their children mixing with young ruffians, or being held back by dull pupils who just do not want to learn.

I am worried, too, as are many of my colleagues. All of our pupils are clever. In the primary schools the children take an examination that tests their English and Arithmetic and measures their intelligence. This is when they are just over eleven, so the examination is called the 'eleven plus'. We take just the top 20 per cent and all the others have to go to Secondary Modern Schools. What frightens us is the thought of teaching 'mixed ability' classes. We have heard of comprehensive schools where children from the very brightest to the very dullest work together. How can those of us teaching foreign languages cope with children who are unable to read and write English? I am afraid for the clever children, too. I know how they stimulate each other, and if they are scattered through a big school they will miss this competition. They will find their work too easy and become bored.

We have had a couple of social occasions for the staffs of the two schools to get to know each other. I asked a man from the Secondary Modern school what he taught. 'Children', he answered, rather curtly. I was a bit puzzled, but realized later that he believed he and his colleagues were more concerned with the children and that we were interested only in our subjects. That, of course, is quite untrue, and it was an unfair thing to say.

The thought of dealing with the older pupils who are not going to take examinations worries me. I have seen them in the town where they are noisy in their behaviour and a bit unruly. How will they react to me? Shall I be able to control them? One pushed into me the other day and when I protested he used a horrible expression. I can't bring myself to repeat it, but I think he meant I should go away.

This is not the end of my fears. How can I ever get used to being one of a community of twelve hundred, rather than three hundred, and one member of staff out of eighty instead of one out of twenty?

Grammar School assembly.

Education

A Secondary Modern Woodwork teacher, 1969

I have been at the Secondary Modern School for six years and I enjoy my job. Woodwork is considered important so it is taught to all boys, and even some of the girls. The more able pupils take the 'O' level examination just as they do at the Grammar School. This happens in all other subjects as well.

Many of the children get good results and go on to further education. One of my boys had a twin brother in the grammar school. They had been separated by the eleven plus, but he was determined to do as well as his brother. In fact, when the 'O' level results came out he had done better! None the less it makes me sad to hear a pupil say, 'If I had any brains I'd have been in the Grammar School', and to hear parents say, 'We were very disappointed when he didn't pass the eleven plus'. This is changing because our examination results are good. Our pupils win craft and technical apprenticeships and even places on sandwich courses and at Polytechnics. Last year an old boy came back to tell us he had an engineering degree.

I am looking forward to the change. It will be good to see the end of separation—'bottling and labelling children' I call it—and to have all pupils in one school, even if it is in two buildings.

There are worries, though. Will our new comprehensive school be like others we have heard about? I know of one head who used to shout from his window, 'Get off the grass you horrible Modern School louts'. A while back I applied for a post in a comprehensive school in another county. While I was sitting in the staffroom for my turn to be interviewed, I remarked on how small it was for such a large staff. One of the teachers present said, 'Oh you won't be in here. This is the staff room for graduates.' One of my colleagues tells a story of a comprehensive school that had to be reorganized, just as ours is going to be. On the first day an eleven year old girl, beautifully clean and in perfect uniform went to the master on duty and asked, 'Please sir, which is the playground for the Grammar School children?'

Will our school have divisions? What sort will they be? I know that the Grammar School staff are to be made Heads of Departments, while our senior people are to have charge of the welfare of children, in years or houses. I wonder how Woodwork will fare in the new school. I have been used to all the children taking practical subjects. Will this continue or will they become second rate subjects for second rate pupils? I once heard a Grammar School teacher say that they gave Cookery to the girls who were too dim to take Latin and anyway the clever ones could always learn it at home. I know there is much more to my subject than sawing, planing and making joints. Clever children can gain a lot from it, and Sixth formers could study Design and

Technology. It will be exciting to see what the more able can do—if I have a chance to teach them. I wonder, too, how the less able will manage in the new school. We have been used to dealing with them, and in our subject especially we have adapted the work to suit them. I don't think the grammar school staff who have never met these children before will be able to present their subjects in a way that will interest and develop those who, through no fault of their own, are not very bright.

We are going to have difficulties, because the school is on two sites. One idea is to divide the children according to ability, but I hope that doesn't happen. It would mean that everything would be the same as it is now, except the name of the school. Another way would be to divide the school according to subjects. That might make more sense because we have excellent craft rooms, while they have plenty of laboratories. It would mean, though, that children would often have to walk a mile through the town to change lessons and you can imagine the problems that will bring. Possibly we could divide the children by their ages, but that would mean the staff having to move between the buildings. I don't see how I can teach my subject in the miserable workshops they have in the Grammar School. I am sure that Comprehensive Schools are the best in theory, but running one on a split site is certainly going to bring headaches.

Education: Conclusion

In the 1980s most secondary schools in Britain are comprehensive. Staff, parents and pupils have accepted the change, and many comprehensive schools are excellent. That, however, is not the end of the story. Schools will always have problems and will have to adapt in order to meet them. The latest development is that the birth rate has been falling so there are fewer children to educate. What difficulties and what opportunities will this bring?

Questions

1. What was done a) by the Education Act of 1902 b) the Education Act of 1944?
2. Why were Comprehensive Schools started?
3. Why was the Grammar School French mistress pleased with her job? What doubts did she have about the new comprehensive school?
4. Why is the Secondary Modern teacher proud of his school? What worries does he have about the new comprehensive school? What changes does he hope to see?
5. Contrast the views of the two teachers.

Classes in a 1960s Secondary Modern School.

4 The Care of the Poor

The Care of the Poor in the Eighteenth Century

In the sixteenth century farmers in some parts of England found they could make a lot of money by selling wool. They gave up growing crops and kept sheep instead. Before this time, they had employed a lot of men, women and children to cultivate their land, but now all they needed was a few shepherds. They gave many of their workers the sack.

If anyone is unemployed today, he just goes to the Department of Health and Social Security where they will let him have some money. In the sixteenth century, though, no-one was bound to help. Sick people, old people and orphan children had to beg, but their neighbours were usually too poor to give them charity, so many died of starvation. Grown men and women, especially the younger ones, became 'vagrants'. That meant they roamed the countryside in gangs, begging, robbing and stealing At first, magistrates had vagrants whipped or branded, but in the end they realized that the best way was to stop people being hungry. How were they to do this?

In 1601 Parliament passed an Act which we now call the Old Poor Law, although, of course, it was new at the time. It said that every parish had to look after its own poor. This was made the duty of the ratepayers who were the wealthier men of the village, such as farmers. Every year they had to elect an Overseer of the Poor. The Overseer collected money from his fellow ratepayers, and used it to help people who had none, or paupers, as they were called. He gave food and clothing to orphans, the sick and the elderly, but paupers who could work had to do so. Usually, they mended the roads.

There was a new problem during the Napoleonic Wars (1793–1815). This was a time of inflation. Prices rose much more quickly than wages, and even people who had work were starving. In many parishes, the Overseers of the Poor made up their wages, so that they could buy enough bread to stay alive. They called this 'bread money'. The idea of

Overseers of the poor. This was a presentation tobacco box to the overseers of one parish, possibly as a reward for their work.

giving bread money was first thought of at Speen in Berkshire, so it is called the Speenhamland System.

The overseer of the poor

I am a farmer here in this village, but I am also overseer. It is not a position I want and nor does anyone else for that matter. The only fair way is for each of us ratepayers to take it in turn to serve for a year, which is what we do. Happily, my time is nearly over, and I shall be glad when it is, I can tell you. There is no pay, of course, and I have had to leave my farm more often than I like to think.

The first thing I did when I became overseer was to assess all the ratepayers. Most of them are farmers like me and they pay a fixed amount per acre. I charged them ten shillings an acre which was a shilling more than last year. They grumbled, of course, but I knew it had been a bad harvest and that most of the labourers would be short of money. Ten shillings an acre is a lot, but I have heard of places where it is a pound an acre or more. That means a farmer's poor rates are as high as his rent. I would give up my farm rather than pay so much.

Once a week I meet the paupers and decide how much money to give them. Some come dressed in rags, complaining that they are starving. There is one widow who is often ill and has a family of small children. Only a man with a heart of stone could refuse to help her. Others don't rely on pity. There are a couple of ruffians in this village who will stop at nothing. The man who was overseer last year refused them and his ricks were fired. A few weeks ago they weren't satisfied with what I gave them, and went away grumbling. They called at my house to ask for more. I showed them the scale the magistrate had drawn up. They had received every penny they were entitled to. That didn't convince them, and they began to threaten me. I sent them packing, but my wife was terrified. She begged me to change my mind, so I called them back and gave them what they wanted.

An overseer has nothing but trouble. The ratepayers grumble because he charges too much, and the paupers grumble because he does not give them enough.

It's a big problem to find something for unemployed labourers to do. Like most parishes we put them on the roads, but it's almost impossible to make sure they are working. I have my farm to run, so I am doing well if I can ride out to the gang a couple of times in the day. They pretend to do something when they see me coming, but I know they stop as soon as my back is turned.

The laziest of these men never want proper jobs. I offered to take on a fellow the other day, but when I told him the wages he just laughed and said he could get nearly as much on the roads. That man will always be a drain on the parish and he could quite well earn his own living.

We have had another problem since the war began. Prices have gone up so fast that even the labourers who have employment cannot earn enough to keep alive. To prevent them from starving, the magistrates of this county introduced the allowance system. They copied it from Berkshire I believe. They say that a man must have two gallons of bread a week, and his wife and children a gallon each. A family of six could well need twelve

Stone breakers. This was the sort of work that overseers would give to poor parishioners.

shillings to buy their bread, but if they have only ten shillings what are they to do? The answer is that they come to the parish and we give them the two shillings to make up their wages. They call it their 'bread money'.

It seemed a good idea at first, but all sorts of things are going wrong. For instance, the system helps the richer farmers. One of my neighbours employs ten men, but he only pays starvation wages—less than that in fact. When they asked for more, he told them to go to the parish. What is the parish? Why, it's just the ordinary rate-payers like me. Except at harvest time I can run my little farm with the help of my family. I have to pay my poor rates, though, and they help my rich neighbours meet their wages bill.

Another difficulty comes from the 'closed' parishes. There are a number of these around here. Each is the property of one landowner, or perhaps two or three who conspire together. They clear the paupers out of their own villages, bribing or bullying them to leave. As soon as a house is empty they pull it down. Now ours is an open parish because there are too many landowners here to agree. The paupers come and live among us. If a farmer wants extra labour at harvest time he can find all he wants here. After the harvest, he sends them back and our ratepayers have to keep them while they are unemployed.

A farm labourer

When we were first married, my wife and I lived quite well. I was a waggoner. I had a good employer who paid me a fair wage. We were able to save money, we rented a cottage and we kept a pig. My wages bought our bread and we sold the pig to pay our rent. My wife worked in the fields at harvest time, and spun cotton the rest of the year. She earned enough to buy us a bit of cheese, and even some meat from time to time. She bought all our clothes as well.

Then came the war and the price of everything

Inside a farm worker's cottage.

just shot up. We could not buy enough bread to keep alive. Another problem was that my wife no longer had any spinning. They tell me it's all done in factories these days. After a while the overseers brought in the allowance system. When I do not earn enough, which is most of the year, I have to ask them for my bread money. To me, that is like going on the parish. I am a proud man and for some time I would not do it. I was determined to earn every penny I had. Some of the other villagers asked me why I was working so hard. 'For myself,' I answered. 'You aren't', they said, 'you are only doing it for the parish'. They used to laugh at me which I found very hard to bear.

In the end my wife and children were close to starving. One of the overseers came to see me and told me I should ask for bread money. I refused and told him I had never been on the parish in my life. He then brought the rector to reason with me, but still I said no. In the end they sent me some money and my wife was so hungry she bought bread with it. Since then I have taken bread money when I have needed it.

A while ago my employer fell on hard times and he had to dismiss me. I'm only a day labourer now, finding work when I can. It doesn't make much difference whether I work one day in the week or six. My family must have bread to eat, and if I don't earn enough to buy it, the parish makes up the difference. Sometimes now I don't look for work as hard as I might.

During the winter, and after the threshing is finished, I may find nothing to do for several weeks. Then I don't just draw bread money, but poor relief. That does make me a true pauper. As such I have to work on the roads. The farmers send carts, picks and shovels, and the overseers tell us where to find stone. We don't do a great deal though, except when we see an overseer coming. They have their farms to run so they can't visit us often. Sometimes we gather fuel in the woods, sometimes we steal a turnip or two out of the fields. We have been poaching, too, for rabbits and pheasants but that is dangerous. Most of the time we just sit around talking. You see we must have our nine shillings a week, whether we do much or little, so what is the point in working?

If you asked me what I really wanted, I would say a fair day's work for a fair day's wages, just like in the old days. I fear they will never return.

Poachers caught in the act.

Questions

1 What did the Poor Law Act of 1601 say?
2 What was the Speenhamland System? What went wrong with it?
3 What was the work of an overseer? What problems might the paupers give him?
4 What were 'closed parishes'?
5 What problems did the farm labourer have? How did the poor law change his character?
6 Where would the overseer and the labourer have agreed?

The Care of the Poor in the Nineteenth Century

During the early part of the nineteenth century, so much money was spent on helping the poor that the government was worried. In 1832 it set up a Royal Commission to find out what was going wrong. The most hard working man on the Commission was Edwin Chadwick.

Chadwick soon discovered all the things you read about in the last section. He decided that the main problem was with people who were quite able to work, but who would rather be on poor relief. How could they be made to earn their own living?

It seemed that George Nicholls, an overseer of the poor from Southwell in Nottinghamshire had the answer to this question. First of all he made sure that life in the local workhouse was thoroughly disagreeable. Then, when poor people went to the Southwell overseers for money, they were not given any. They were told there was no need to starve as they could live in the workhouse. The workhouse was so unpleasant that only those who were desperate would go there. Anyone who could find a job did so. It was soon clear who really was in need and who was shamming. People called this the 'workhouse test'.

Chadwick and the other members of the Royal Commission thought George Nicholls's scheme was so good that they persuaded Parliament to make it the rule for the whole country. This was done by the Poor Law Amendment Act of 1834.

As many parishes were too poor to build workhouses on their own, they joined together in groups of about twenty called Poor Law Unions. The

This cartoon goes to extremes, but conditions were certainly worse for paupers after the Poor Law Amendment Act of 1834.

men in charge were Poor Law Guardians. Like the overseers they were elected by the ratepayers, but there was much less for them to do. A Union was rich enough to pay a full time workhouse master, and a staff to help him.

George Nicholls of Southwell

Until we introduced our new system in 1822, the paupers of Southwell were a constant trouble to us. When they came to collect their relief, many of them would threaten the overseer, and some even attacked him. I have seen a woman seize money from the pay table and make off with it, saying she would have it no matter what the overseer said. What was perhaps worse, the poor of the town were developing all sorts of bad habits. Parents were ill-treating their children, mothers were neglecting their homes and there was a lot of drunkenness. The poor had lost any idea that their earnings should depend on how much work they did. Also, they never thought of looking after themselves or saving money. It had become the duty of the parish to make up their wages, and to help them if they were in need.

The whole problem lay with the allowance system. It meant that a man was better off as a pauper, living on the parish, than he was as a labourer earning his own living. I am not surprised that so few of the people wanted to work, and that so many of them became paupers.

Then, in 1822, we abolished the allowance system. No-one was allowed out-door relief, but paupers had, instead, to live in the workhouse, Here they were fed and treated properly, but there were certain strict rules. These were the most important:

1. Men and women lived separately, even husbands and wives
2. No visitors were allowed, and no-one could go out unless it was to leave for good.
3. There was to be no smoking or drinking.
4. There was plenty of hard work, such as breaking bones.

Our whole aim was to make the pauper worse off than the labourer living on his own earnings. In this we succeeded, so if anyone applies to the parish for relief we are able to apply the 'workhouse test'. We refuse them money, but offer them a place in the workhouse instead. Now, either they are in real need or they are not. If they are, they come into the workhouse. If they are not, they go away and find work.

I'll tell you what happened to three men who came to our workhouse. The first was immediately violent and sulky. He said he would never break bones for the parish when he could earn money breaking stones for others. He went out the next day. The second said it hurt his back to bend so much and that he would leave at once, which he did. The third had a hole to dig which he disliked so much that he very soon left. He had been one of the most troublesome men in the parish, but he went off quietly. He said he did not complain of the food, or the accommodation, but if he had to work, then he was going to work for himself. He now gets his own living in a brickyard, by threshing wheat, and any odd job he can find.

Indeed, there has been a change in character in all the poor of Southwell. It shows itself in a number of ways. A good many keep pigs, which they did not do before, because if they had done so, they could not have claimed money from the parish. They rent bits of land for gardening, which they do in their

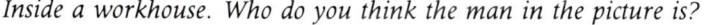
Inside a workhouse. Who do you think the man in the picture is?

The Care of the Poor

spare time. Their houses are better furnished. The men spend less time in the ale-house and more with their families. They are much prouder, scorning the paupers who live off the parish. They bring up their children to feel the same way. Many who used to hate the overseer, no longer do so. They are saving money and place it with the savings' bank of which he is secretary. These people are pleased to tell anyone how much they have put by.

It is not only the poor who have benefited: the ratepayers have as well. In the last ten years of the old system, the poor rates at Southwell were nearly £14,000. In the first ten years of the new system, they were £4,000.

A country parson

When the Poor Law Amendment Act was passed it seemed to be a wise measure. I felt that the ratepayers must gain, and that the poor themselves would once more become thrifty and hard working. Well, much good has been done for the ratepayers since the cost of poor relief is much less than it was. For the poor themselves, the results have been far from happy. The workhouse now casts a shadow over their lives. It is always in the background as a constant threat. They know they may one day have to go to that dreaded place because of a misfortune which is no fault of their own. It might be sickness, unemployment, or the death of a husband. Nearly all poor people expect to spend their last years in the workhouse.

You can have some idea what the presence of the workhouse means to them, just by looking at the one in our parish. It is a large, heavy building, with solid wings jutting out from the main body, so that the court is cold and dark. On one side is a garden, so gloomy that it reminds me of a graveyard. There is not a flower, not a rose bush, not even a currant bush. There are are just straight lines of vegetables, potatoes, cabbages, onions and beans. Usually, one or two old men are to be seen there working dispiritedly. Everything about the place looks solid and useful, yet it is dreary, dark and cold. There are children in the court, but they are not playing happily as children should, and all is silent.

The building is kept clean and tidy. Everyone has enough clothes and food and they have fires during the winter. If a family is homeless, it can come here. If anyone is sick, a doctor will see him and give him medicine. If a man grows too old to look after himself, he will be cared for. The workhouse master and his staff are never deliberately cruel and, as they always do, the poor show great kindness to each other. Yet the very sight of the workhouse is unpleasant. It makes me think of sickness, old age, extreme poverty and every kind of misery.

I know the poor feel the same as I do. There was an old man who lost his job and asked the Guardians for relief. Instead, they offered him a place in the workhouse. He said he would rather die than go there. Within a week he was found dead from starvation. I have heard of folk who committed small crimes when they had no money to buy bread. They would rather be sent to prison than have to go to the workhouse.

One of the rules is that males and females shall be separated from each other, and this can be very cruel, especially when it is applied to children. One little boy tore out his hair in handfuls at being taken from his mother. It is also very hard on the elderly. There was an old couple, both over seventy, who were in need. They asked for a small sum of money, but the Guardians refused and sent them to the workhouse. At once they were separated. Neither of them could eat the workhouse food, and the old man complained that he missed his cup of tea in the evening with his wife. They could not bear it, so they left.

I must tell you, too, about Tom Carderey. He was a cheerful old fellow who made a living as a rat-catcher and a broom-maker. One day the roof of his house fell in, and he asked the Guardians for some money to repair it. They decided that the walls of the house would not support a new roof, so they took Tom and his wife into the workhouse. The disgrace was too much for Tom. His spirit was quite broken and it was not long before he died.

Christmas dinner in the workhouse. How far does this cheerful scene fit in with the parson's account?

The Care of the Poor

Stone breaking in a workhouse.

Samuel Green, an inmate of Andover workhouse

I am employed in the workhouse at bone breaking for most of the time. I have seen a great many marrow bones brought in, some of them were beef, some mutton and some bacon. We look out for the fresh bones and then we are like a parcel of dogs after them. Some men are not as particular about the bones being fresh as others. I like the fresh bones. The marrow is as good as the raw meat: it is all covered over by the bone and no filth can get at it. I have picked a sheep's head, a mutton bone and a beef bone that were fresh and good. Sometimes I have had one that was stale and stunk, and I ate it even then. I ate it because I was hungry. You see, we only have bread and gruel for breakfast, and as there is no bread allowed for dinner on meat days, we save our bread from breakfast. Then having had only gruel for breakfast, we are hungry before dinner time. A pint and a half of gruel is not much for a man's breakfast, so to satisfy our hunger we eat the stale and stinking meat.

I even saw a man named Reeves eat horse flesh off the bone. I told him it was horse flesh but he did not care: it went down as sweet as a nut. I once quarrelled with Reeves about eating horse flesh and he asked what odds his eating it was to me. I said it was no odds to me, but I could not think how he could be so nasty as to eat such stuff.

Questions

1. What did Edwin Chadwick think was the main weakness of the Poor Law?
2. What did the Poor Law Amendment Act of 1832 say?
3. What changes did George Nicholls make at Southwell? What good results did he claim?
4. Describe a workhouse. Which people suffered most from its strict rules? Was this what Chadwick and Nicholls intended?
5. What happened at Andover workhouse?

The Care of the Poor in the Twentieth Century

Towards the end of the nineteenth century many people realized that men like Edwin Chadwick had been mistaken. There were very few work dodgers. Most adults who were unemployed badly wanted to find jobs, so it was wrong to punish them. Almost all poor people could not work anyway. They were too young, too old, or too ill. Boards of Guardians became less stony-hearted. For example, they no longer kept orphan children in the workhouses. Instead, they put small groups in ordinary houses and paid married couples to look after them. That meant they had, as nearly as possible, a normal family life.

However, it was not enough for Guardians to be kind, for they did not have enough money to give the poor all they needed. In the early twentieth century the government decided to help. The cabinet minister who made the changes was David Lloyd George.

In 1908, Lloyd George started Old Age Pensions for people over seventy. The pension was only five shillings (25p) a week, but in those days that would pay the food bills.

Then, in 1911, Lloyd George started a National Insurance scheme. If a worker was sick he had ten shillings a week, and free medical treatment. The money for all this came from a special fund. Each worker had to pay fourpence a week, his employers had to pay threepence for him, and the government paid twopence. That was a total of ninepence, or less than 4p in modern money. Everyone was glad to have help when they were sick. However they did not want to pay their contributions, even though Lloyd George said they were having 'ninepence for fourpence'. He was Welsh, and one day a crowd of servant girls gathered outside his house shouting, 'Taffy was a Welshman, Taffy was a thief'.

To help the unemployed Lloyd George opened Labour Exchanges and started the dole. A worker who lost his job went to a Labour Exchange where they either found him another, or if this wasn't possible, paid him some money. Unfortunately, the dole was only for people in a few important industries like building and engineering. Parliament thought unemployment benefit for everyone would be far too expensive. The result was that many who were out of work still had to go the to Boards of

You had to be earning less than £31 a year to get the first old age pension, but it was the start of a social revolution.

Guardians for help. As we have seen, they did not have enough money to do much.

An engineer in the 1930s

I am a pattern maker and I served a seven year apprenticeship to learn my trade. I suppose it's not too bad to be unemployed if you are only fit for labouring, but I've got all this skill in my hands and I can't use it. I'm no better off than a navvy.

When I first lost my job it didn't seem too bad. I would wake in the morning and go to get up as usual. Then I would realize I could have a nice lie-in. It was like being on holiday. That didn't last, though. The days went by and I got desperate. I cycled all over the place, and I stood in queues with scores of men knowing that only a couple of us would be lucky and get work. Many a time I was outside a factory gate at six o'clock in the morning, hoping to catch the foreman's eye. It was useless. I am fifty-eight you see, and no-one wants a man that age. After a time I gave up really trying. I strolled

'Signing on' at the Labour Exchange.

around the factories, but it was just force of habit. I knew the answer would be 'no', so there was little point in worrying.

I don't bother at all now. I get up late, about nine o'clock. Sometimes I do odd jobs around the house, though its hard to find the money for paint or a piece of wood. Sometimes I do a bit of gardening. With all the spare time you might think I could enjoy myself. The trouble is, I am too miserable. I like a drop of beer, but if I drink much of that the wife goes hungry. I can afford a cheap seat at the cinema about once a fortnight and I find a few pennies to do the football pools. I day dream a lot about what I will do if I have a big win. Mostly, I just go with my mates and we stand on the street corner. We gossip and we watch the people go by. It's as good a way of passing the time as any.

I am used to the idea that no-one wants me now. Life would be bearable if only I wasn't so short of money. At first I had the dole. I had paid my stamp money for years, and thought I was insured for as long as I was unemployed, but they told me at the Labour Exchange that I could only have dole for six months. After that I thought I would have to go on poor relief. It didn't happen but the scheme they brought in was nearly as bad. They give us 'transitional benefits'. It's barely enough to live on and if that isn't bad enough, we have to have a means test. The Public Assistance Committee employs a lot of snoopers and spies. One of them came to my house as soon as I put in for my transitional benefits. I had a little silver cup I had won for boxing as a boy, and he docked me half a crown a week until I had sold it and spent the money. 'You can't expect to draw the full benefit while you have silverware in the house', he said.

My youngest boy got a paper round and earned himself a shilling a week. We were very pleased as we thought that at least he would be able to afford a few sweets and a comic. The Public Assistance heard about it though and docked me the shilling. My wife's sister gave her a coat. It looked quite new and it wasn't long before there was a man round asking where we had found the money to buy it.

The time was when my wife kept this house spotless. She used to shine up the kitchen range, polish the doorknobs and keep our front doorstep the whitest in the road. She doesn't have the energy now. She spends all her time worrying about money. Every penny counts, you see. All we can afford is food like bread, margarine, potatoes and a little jam and tea. At times I feel I would give anything for a really tasty meal, even if it was only fish and chips with plenty of salt and vinegar. None of us gets the proper food we should. We always seem to be catching coughs and colds.

My wife and I have talked about moving. My brother says there are sometimes jobs going down in London, where he lives. I don't think I could risk it, though. I saw a young couple tramping south the other day. They went into a café to buy a cup of tea. They had a baby with them and they fed it from the bottle. It looked to me as if there was only water in the bottle. I couldn't take to the road with my family. Besides, what if I didn't find work in London? It's bad enough being out of work here among folk we know. It would be unbearable among all those unfriendly people down there.

I suppose I shall see sixty-five, though it's many, long dull years away. I shall draw my old age pension then, though it's not much to look forward to. It will be less than I am getting now.

A man who went on the Hunger March

I come from Jarrow and I worked all my life in Palmer's shipyard. Most of the men in Jarrow worked there as well. Then, in 1933 they closed it and threw 8,000 of us on the dole. There were five men for every single job in the town. We didn't know what we could do about it. We heard of the National Unemployed Workers' Movement, but it seemed to be run by communists. They caused a lot of trouble, like the riots against the means test in Birkenhead. We didn't want to do anything like that.

Then, in 1935, we had a new M.P., Ellen Wilkinson. She is just a little slip of a woman, red-headed and pretty, but she is a lively one. She got together with the mayor and they decided to organize a march to London. Two hundred of us volunteered. People gave us money, so we each had £2 for our expenses, as well as some leather and nails to mend our boots. The Boy Scouts lent us some field kitchens to cook our meals midday, and we had an old bus for all the kit. We carried a big banner with the words 'Jarrow Crusade' at the head of the column, but the most important thing we took was an oak box with our petition asking Parliament to find work for Jarrow. Twelve thousand people had signed it.

We set out at the beginning of October 1936. There was a service before we left, and the Bishop of Jarrow gave us his blessing. The town band came with us for a couple of miles, but after that the only music we had was mouthorgans. Still, we marched in step, just like soldiers. It reminded me of when I went to France during the war.

It was 300 miles to London and we aimed to get there in a month. We soon found ten miles a day was plenty, because most of us hadn't eaten properly for years. We had blisters, too. There were some medical students with us who patched up our feet. Ellen used to help them. She was marvellous. She had to leave us once in a while for business, but she marched most of the way with us.

All along the route people turned out to see us, and lots of them clapped and cheered, but we never knew for certain if we would be welcome. The people of York wouldn't let us into the town. Sometimes we had to sleep on the bare floor and all we were given to eat was bread and marge. At other places we had good cooked meals, and the tables were laid with cloths and proper cutlery. At Leicester the men in the Co-operative boot factory stayed up all night mending our boots. We knew Harrogate was full of snobs and we didn't expect

The Jarrow marchers.

much there, but some officers of the Territorial Army met us, and they couldn't have been kinder.

We marched into London during a thunderstorm. We held a meeting, all very orderly, and we were so well behaved they let us into the House of Commons to have tea. On November 3rd, Ellen gave our petition to Parliament. The Prime Minister, Stanley Baldwin, didn't have much to say, while the President of the Board of Trade, Walter Runciman, even pretended things were getting better in Jarrow. From that day to this, the government has done nothing.

We took the train back to Jarrow. When we got home, the clerks at the Labour Exchange docked our benefits. They said that if any jobs had come up while were away, we wouldn't have been there to take them.

The modern equivalent of the Jarrow March.

The Care of the Poor: Conclusion

The Welfare State. It was not the government that cured unemployment but the Second World War (1939–1945). It created jobs for everyone. When it was over the country prospered for many years, so few people were out of work. Also, between 1945 and 1950, Parliament passed a number of laws which established what we call the Welfare State. Now, anyone who is ill can have free medical treatment and sick pay. Moreover, a person who is unemployed can have the dole. Even people who are not covered by national insurance can have enough money from Social Security to live reasonably well.

Unemployment returned to Britain in the late 1970s, and by early 1981 almost 2½ million people were out of work. Thanks to the dole and Social Security benefits there was none of the dreadful hardship of the 1930s, but there was a good deal of unhappiness. Many businesses, even well organized ones, went bankrupt, while others, not quite as unfortunate, had to make large numbers of their employees redundant. A lot of middle aged men, who had held important positions, and who had given their firms excellent service, found they were not wanted any more. Though it was no fault of their own, almost all found it humiliating to have to stand in the dole queue. Some were too ashamed to tell their families. They went on leaving home and returning at the same times, every day, and pretended they had been at work.

Others who suffered badly were the school leavers. For example, there were many boys who enjoyed woodwork and hoped to become carpenters or joiners. They found the building trade was so slack that absolutely no-one wanted them as apprentices. A small number became shopfitters, but the rest had to look elsewhere. Even then, they were lucky to find anything at all. The government started training schemes and job creation schemes, but they only lasted a few months. Many more young people went on with their education after they were sixteen, but they could not remain students for ever.

It is possible that we shall never again have full employment, and that many of us must learn to be happy without a job. This will not be easy. For centuries people have believed that it was somehow immoral to be one of the 'idle rich' or even worse, one of the 'idle poor'. It will be a long time before we have as much respect for someone who is unemployed as we do for someone who is in work.

Questions

1. What measures were introduced by David Lloyd George?
2. How did unemployment change the character of the engineer and his wife?
3. Why was Jarrow especially unfortunate in the 1930s?
4. What was the purpose of the Jarrow Crusade? Why did it fail?
5. What do we mean by the 'Welfare State'?
6. What problems were there in the early 1980s? Why did the unemployed suffer less than in the 1930s?

5 Law and Order

Law and Order in the Eighteenth Century

Police. In the eighteenth century it was the duty of each parish to police itself. Every year, the ratepayers met and chose one of their number to be constable. He did the job, unpaid, for twelve months, when someone else had to take a turn. Constables were not usually efficient, partly because they had no salaries, and partly because they had their own jobs to do, or their businesses or farms to run.

In the villages constables might just about cope on their own, but in the towns it was impossible. There, they usually had a force of paid watchmen who patrolled the streets, and all the constable had to do was supervise them. The watch could have been efficient, but the wages were so low that the only men who would join were those who were too old to earn a living in ordinary work.

Since the police forces were inefficient, the government tried to frighten people into good behaviour with savage punishments, like flogging, branding, transportation or hanging. At one time there were 200 crimes for which you could be hanged. Some of them were quite trivial, like damaging a fish pond. However, since criminals knew there was very little chance of being caught, these punishments did not deter them.

Only in London were there any proper police. This was the force based on Bow Street and which is described in the case study.

Prisons. Today we look on prisons as places where criminals are sent for punishment and to be reformed. In the eighteenth century they were rather for storing people, much as we would use a cupboard for china. Some of the inmates were suspected criminals who were waiting to be tried. Others were convicted criminals who were waiting for one of the punishments already described. Most were not criminals at all, but debtors. In those days if you were in debt, you could be sent to prison

Two young 'blades' attacking a 'Charley' or nightwatchman.

until you, or one of your friends, paid what you owed.

Most prisons were run by gaolers who had no salaries, and who made any money they could out of their prisoners. Very little was spent on the buildings, which were usually filthy, and without sanitation or clean water.

One man who was very concerned about prisons was John Howard. He visited a great many and described what he had seen in his 'State of the Prisons' published in 1777. It was a horrifying book, but very few reforms were made until the nineteenth century.

John Fielding and the Bow Street Police

My name is John Fielding and I am a London magistrate. I cannot see, so people call me the 'blind beak'. I can promise you, though, that I am quite able to do my work. I never forget a voice. I remember voices better than most people remember names. No criminal can persuade me he is a first offender, if I have ever tried him before.

My house is in Bow Street. Not only do I live there, but there is also a court room and a lock-up. There is a police office, too, as I will explain.

It was my half brother Henry, the novelist, who first came to Bow Street as a magistrate, back in 1748. I was appointed myself two years later. We did all the usual work of magistrates, such as keeping an eye on the constables, hoping to make sure they did their work, which most of them did not. We also questioned people who had been arrested, and, of course, we tried them if it seemed at all likely they were guilty. I am happy to say, that in one important way, Henry and I were very different from other magistrates. We never took bribes. Some of our colleagues were what is known as 'trading justices' and they made a lot of money dishonestly. We scorned to do that.

It did not take us long to realize that even if all the magistrates did their work properly, crime in London would not end. We decided to employ detectives.

You will know that constables serve, unpaid, for a year, and do not give up their ordinary work. As a result, we knew quite a number who had held office. We went to the best of them and asked if they would like to be full-time detectives or Bow Street Runners as we called them. Many agreed. We had a little government money, so we were able to pay each a man a guinea a week. A good runner can earn far more than that, however. To encourage people to arrest criminals, the government will pay a reward of up to £40 for everyone that is arrested and convicted. Runners have a good chance of earning these rewards. We also release them from time to time to do private work. If there is a burglary in a big house in the country, the owner knows it is a waste of time to tell the village constable, so he will send for a Bow Street Runner, and if one is free we let him go. He can earn as much as a guinea a day in private work, as well as claiming expenses.

Some people dislike my Runners and are very critical of them. They say they spend so much time

A Bow Street Runner, Mr Townsend.

with evil-doers that they must be rogues themselves. I agree that very often Runners are to be found drinking in low ale houses, with bad company, but they can only do their job properly by mixing with criminals. These wicked characters know far more of crime than honest folk, and they are often willing to talk, for a reward, or because they have quarrelled among themselves.

To my great sorrow Henry died in 1754 but I have gone on with our work. The Runners were successful, but I decided more needed to be done. In 1763, I organized patrols, both horse and foot. They have a uniform which is a black top hat, blue great coat and trousers, white gloves and a red waistcoat. Because of the waistcoat, people call them 'robin redbreasts'.

Obviously these uniformed men are not detectives. They patrol regular beats, and their job is to keep order and prevent crime. The foot patrol goes as far as seven miles beyond Charing Cross, and the horse patrol for some ten miles further. They have done well. For example, Hounslow Heath is now safe for travellers. Not long ago few dared cross it at night because of highwaymen.

The great problem is that London is growing too fast, and my men are too few. If there were a few more offices like mine at Bow Street, I am sure that London would be a law-abiding city.

John Fielding, the 'Blind Beak'

Law and Order

John Howard, prison reformer

I took no interest in prisons until I reached the age of 47. That was in 1773 when I became Sheriff of Bedford. As Sheriff, I was also a magistrate, and I was both amazed and disturbed to see prisoners who had been found innocent at their trials, dragged back to gaol. When I asked the reason, I was told it was because they had not paid their fees. The gaoler, it seemed, had no salary, so he made what money he could from his wretched captives. The prison had a whole scale of fees, for discharge, for putting on irons, for taking them off, and so on. Anyone who could not pay his fees remained in prison until someone took pity on him, and paid them for him.

I then went to inspect the prison and was horrified at the squalor and the misery I found. I asked myself whether Bedford gaol was alone in this, or whether others were the same. Since then I have spent my time travelling Britain, and the continent of Europe, visiting prisons everywhere. Some are indeed better than Bedford gaol, but many are far worse.

The Sussex County Gaol at Horsham is well ordered. The Duke of Richmond took much interest in the new building, which was finished in 1779. Each felon has his own room, ten feet by seven, with a bedstead and two blankets. There is also a fireplace, and an allowance of coals for the winter. The prison has a courtyard where the felons may go during the day. It has a pump with a well of pure water.

When a felon arrives, he is washed and given a green striped uniform, two shirts, two pairs of stockings, and a pair of shoes. The food is only bread and water, but at least there is enough of it. The loaves have to be weighed and I saw that each was a good two pounds.

The County Bridewell at Wymondham in Norfolk is very different. The male prisoners have a day room with three bedrooms leading off it. The bedrooms are little more than cupboards, about six feet by four. A prisoner complained to me that he had to sleep in one of these with two boys who had a most unpleasant skin disease. The women have another room, and when I visited there were four poor sick creatures in it, with padlocks on their legs. There is also a dungeon down eight steps. It is arched with brick, has a dirt floor and contains some stocks. The only light comes through two small holes in the ceiling. There are no beds. The prisoners sleep on straw which is so old that it is worn almost to dust.

A big problem at Wymondham is that the prison is not secure. There is a big courtyard, but the gaoler dares not let the prisoners use it, for fear they

King's Bench Prison, London. At some prisons, like this, visitors were allowed at all hours.

might escape. Most of the time they are not only locked indoors, but in irons. It is much cheaper to buy irons than it would be to rebuild the prison.

The great evil is that, save for a few places like Horsham, the gaolers have no salaries. They make what money they can from the fees they charge and from the sale of food, drink and other items which they sell to the prisoners. I have found wealthy prisoners living in comfort, able to have all they want, though at enormous cost. A prisoner who has no money, however, will suffer horribly, chained in some dark, dirty cell, trying to live on the bread allowance the county gives him. This is only a penny loaf, and some prisoners will eat a two day allowance for one breakfast. The worst treated are those who have money but will not buy from the gaoler. One such man was kept alone in a dark cell, chained to a dead body.

Prisoners who are locked up for days, surrounded by their own filth, are bound to sicken. A sturdy young labourer may have his health ruined after a few weeks in one of these places. The most dreaded disease is gaol-fever which may carry off not only the prisoners, but their gaolers and even judges and jurymen as well.

Prisons not only breed disease, but they also breed evil, and that is far worse. The young and innocent are thrust together with prostitutes and hardened criminals. It is almost impossible for anyone to go to gaol and not emerge with a worse character than he had when he was admitted.

Questions

1 How was the police organized in the eighteenth century? How did the government try to make up for its inefficiency?
2 What police work did magistrates do? How were the Fieldings different?
3 What police forces did the Fieldings organize?
4 How were prisons used in the main? How were they organized?
5 What did John Howard find was wrong with the prisons of his day?

Hogarth's view of the inside of a prison. This man is a debtor, and it seems that he has been unable to escape his worries inside!

Law and Order in the Nineteenth Century

Police. In the eighteenth and early nineteenth centuries a good many people disliked the idea of having a police force because they were afraid it would interfere with their freedom. They thought of 'police' as we would think of 'secret police'. However, in 1829, the Home Secretary, Sir Robert Peel, persuaded Parliament to pass the Metropolitan Police Act. This created a force of police for those parts of London covered by the Bow Street Foot Patrol. This was disbanded as were the parish constables and the watch, though the Bow Street Runners and Horse Patrol remained.

At first people were against the New Police, but by 1839 they had proved themselves, so Parliament passed another Act giving them control of all of London except the City. The Bow Street Horse Patrol became the mounted branch, but the Runners were disbanded. The reason was that the two Police Commissioners, Sir Charles Rowan and Richard Mayne believed that the duty of the police was to prevent crime. In the end they did agree to employ some detectives, but there were very few until Rowan and Mayne retired.

Later, in 1856, Parliament passed another Act which gave all the counties police forces, modelled on the one in London.

'Peelers' were not popular at first. Many people saw them as no better than criminals.

Prisons. When John Howard died, people like Elizabeth Fry went on with his work, and during the nineteenth century, much was done to reform the prisons. Buildings were clean and secure, each had a Governor and warders, all of whom had salaries, and prisoners were properly fed. Even more important, attempts were made to reform criminals. There were two methods. One was the 'separate system' under which prisoners were kept in solitary confinement. In the end, this would break the most hardened criminal, and the prison chaplain then had the chance to persuade him to begin a new life. The other was the 'silent system' under which prisoners lived together but were not allowed to speak. They were given useless, disagreeable work such as oakum picking, turning the treadwheel, or digging holes and then filling them in again. It was hoped that this would frighten them into good behaviour.

A common way of dealing with criminals in the nineteenth century was to transport them to Australia. There they were given to farmers who used them almost as slaves until their sentences were finished. The Australians welcomed the convicts at first because they were short of labour. Later, though, they objected to their country being used as a dumping ground for British criminals. Transportation gradually came to an end in the middle years of the century.

Sir Charles Rowan and the New Police

I fought in the war in Spain under the Duke of Wellington. I was commander of the 52nd Regiment, and my troops were no ordinary ones, for they were light infantry. Unlike the regiments of the line who fight shoulder to shoulder, light infantry nearly always work on their own, or in small groups. At all times they must be ready to think and act for themselves. You will realize, of course, the discipline of the curse, flog and hang kind was no use to us. We depended on mutual trust and respect, so punishments were almost unknown. From my army days I learnt this simple truth: it is far better to prevent a man from doing something wrong, than it is to let him commit an offence, and then punish him afterwards.

What is true for soldiers must also be true for civilians. We have had so much crime in England because we have relied on fear of punishment—branding, transportation and hanging. Horrible though they are, these punishments have failed to deter criminals. What must be done is to prevent crime in the first place.

When, in 1829, Sir Robert Peel asked me to be one of the Commissioners of the New Police, I was pleased to accept, for I wanted to try out my ideas. I stated firmly in my book of General Instructions that it should be understood from the first that the main job of the police is the prevention of crime. Officers and Police Constables must therefore try to be so active and hard working that anyone would find it very difficult to commit a crime within the part of the town under their control.

The New Police were to have charge of the Metropolitan area—not the City of London, but a belt around it, its limits varying from three to seven miles from Charing Cross. We divided it into seventeen divisions, and to every division we allocated a Company. In every Company we have a total of 144 police. They are organized into sections, nine strong, each with a sergeant in charge. There is an Inspector to command every group of four sections, and a Superintendent to command the entire Company. The whole of a Division is divided into beats, and there is a constable to patrol every one of them. There is not a street, nor even a court or an alley where a constable does not appear at some time or other.

A constable must do more than patrol, of course. He must get to know the honest people on his beat, and win their trust. He must also get to know the criminals and keep an eye on them.

I must confess that there have been problems. A constable's pay is only a guinea a week, whereas a skilled worker or a clerk can earn thirty shillings. The result is that the best men do not join the police force. The downfall of many of our constables is drink. Hardly a pay-day goes by without one or two of them being reprimanded or dismissed for being drunk on duty.

The public have not been helpful. Too many people think the police wish to take away their liberty. One of my constables asked the driver of a nobleman's carriage to keep to the left of the road. The nobleman told his footman to knock the

From the beginning the police have been suspicious of loiterers.

constable to the ground and then ordered the coachman to drive the carriage backwards and forwards over him. Once, when a riot seemed likely, I gathered a force of police to prevent it. The next day there were posters all over London saying Peel's bloody gang was to be armed with cutlasses and calling a public meeting to protest. Even magistrates are hostile. A gang threw one of my constables on to some spiked railings, and all that happened was that their leader was fined £1.

I do not intend to change my principles I can assure you. Even after 1829 the Bow Street office remained and its runners still plied their useless trade as detectives. They ignored us and we ignored them. In 1839, I'm happy to say, all the police in London came under our control. We at once sacked all of the runners. Under no circumstances will I have detectives at Scotland Yard.

A visitor to the boys' prison at Tothill Fields

This prison is meant for boys up to the age of sixteen. Most of them are over twelve, but some are as young as six. They seemed to need a nurse, rather than a warder. Yet everything here is much as it is in the prisons for adults, such as Cold Bath Fields. There is a Prison Governor, there are warders with their great bunches of keys, and their cutlasses, and there is a prison van to bring the young criminals from court. In every way the treatment of our young prisoners is the same as that of adult offenders.

I asked some of the boys what they had done wrong.

'Heaving an oyster shell through a street lamp', said one.

'He has been here three times before', said the warder. 'He probably committed the offence just to get another month's shelter here.'

'And you?', I asked another.

'A woman said I hit her baby.'

'And you?'

'Heaving clay.'

This last one had been here fourteen times before. 'But mostly for cadging', said the boy indignantly, 'only twice or three times for prigging.'

One little fellow of eight had been sentenced to fourteen days and a flogging. His only offence had been to steal eight plums from an orchard.

I could not help feeling that these wretches were being punished more for being street urchins than for their crimes. The magistrates who sentenced them must have behaved in just the same way when they were boys.

Some of the prisoners, it is true, are already hardened criminals. A lad of sixteen in prison for the eleventh time told me his story.

'I've been at prigging for about four years. I had one calendar month here for a pair of boots. Then I stole a box of silver pencil cases from a jeweller's shop. I got four calendar months for that. Then I was took for two bundles of cigars and had one month here. After that I was took for some meerschaum pipes and had another month.'

I asked what he meant to do when he was free

Mealtime at Tothill Fields Boys' Prison.

again. He replied that he would go on thieving as he had no other way of getting a living.

At Tothill Fields they use the silent system. Just as in a prison for adults, the boys are not allowed to talk in case they should teach one another bad habits. Also they have to do hard, disagreeable work in the hope that this will frighten them from committing any more crimes. Mostly this is 'oakum picking'. They sit together on benches. Each has a hook strapped to his knee and a measured quantity of old rope at his side. Firstly, he unravels a length and then he draws the pieces backwards and forwards in the hook to loosen them. Finally, he pulls all the fibres apart with his finger nails. No-one is allowed to speak, the air is full of dust, and the boys' hands are red and raw. No work could be more unpleasant. Children under nine have to pick a pound of oakum a day, and lads of sixteen twice as much. The oakum is sold for a trifling sum to make coconut matting.

Five hours a day are spent picking oakum, one hour and three-quarters are allowed for meals, and one hour and three-quarters for school, and there is

Pentonville Prison, built in 1840.

an hour of exercise. The rest of the time the boys are locked in their cells.

I visited the school room. Some of the boys read easily enough, but half of those who were sixteen could not read the simple sentence 'The old man must be led by the hand or he may fall in the deep pit'. Their only book was the Bible.

There was a text on the wall of the school room which read, 'I will arise and go to my Father and say unto Him, "Father I have sinned against Heaven and before Thee"'. Later, however, when I saw some prisoners being discharged, I fear there was not one parent come to collect any of them.

Working the water engine was one of the prisoners' duties

Questions

1 What did the Metropolitan Police Acts of 1829 and 1839 say? What happened to the older police forces?
2 What were Rowan's ideas on law and order?
3 What problems did the New Police have?
4 How were prisons improved in the nineteenth century?
5 Explain the separate system, the silent system, transportation.
6 For what offences might children be sent to prison? How were they treated there?

Law and Order in the Twentieth Century

Police. If you had asked anyone living in the nineteenth century what the main causes of crime were, they would probably have answered, 'poverty and ignorance'. It was believed that if only everyone had enough to eat, and had a good education, there would be no more criminals. Today, no-one goes hungry, and all children go to school, but crime is a bigger problem that it has ever been.

There is more violence, such as 'baby bashing', brawling in pubs and discos, and disorders at football matches. In the 1970s it became the fashion to have large numbers of pickets during strikes, so that armies of police were needed to control them. Politics are another source of trouble. Parades and demonstrations often end in fights. In Northern Ireland, and even in Britain, there are bombings from time to time.

Professional criminals are flourishing as well. As soon as they find one type of crime ceases to pay, they turn to another. Many of them are very expert.

A great deal of police time, well over 10 per cent, is spent in dealing with traffic offences and road accidents. These were rare in the days of horse drawn vehicles, but now they are common. Someone is killed on the roads of Britain every hour, and someone is injured every minute and a half.

The police today use modern methods and equipment. For example, they have computers and forensic scientists to help them. They manage to solve about 40 per cent of the crimes reported to them. However, they feel there are not enough police, that they have too much work to do, and that the public does not show them enough appreciation or respect.

Prisons. In the prisons, it has been recognized for a long time that neither the 'separate system' nor the 'silent system' did much good. The separate system with its solitary confinement was more likely to drive criminals insane than to reform them: the silent system with its degrading work meant they left prison even more bitter than when they arrived. Now there all kinds of social workers to help criminals. Young offenders have special treatment. They have their own courts while, if they are sent away, it is to an approved school, which is quite unlike a prison.

Riot shields are a sign of the times.

The prison service, though, is under strain. Most buildings are over a hundred years old, and even worse, they are badly overcrowded. Many prison staff feel that their task is hopeless and are losing heart.

A modern policeman

There is a song that says 'A policeman's lot is not a happy one'. I believe W. S. Gilbert wrote it about a hundred years ago. He didn't know the half of it.

One of our main duties is to prevent crime. How are we supposed to do that? You cannot tell a criminal just by his appearance, though I have often been asked, 'Do I look like a criminal, officer?' In many ways it was easier in the old days when I first joined the force. A bobby on the beat really knew his area and its people. The public were used to seeing him and felt they could rely on him. Racing around in a panda car you don't get to know the local folk in the same way as before. It does mean you can get to the scene of a crime or accident much more quickly of course.

Crime is growing at a fantastic rate, especially among the young. It used to be thought that if people had enough to eat, they wouldn't steal. I don't think anyone goes hungry these days, but there is more stealing than ever. It's easy to see why shop lifting has increased. A modern store is like an Aladdin's cave. The goods are made to look as tempting as possible and it's all self-service. The shop-keepers want people to take things they don't really need, but they complain when the customer leaves without paying.

There are new crimes, too. Whoever heard of baby bashing in the old days? It is all too common now. Social workers say it is the parents' way of crying for help. They don't seem to worry about the baby crying. One of the most frustrating things these days is that folk seem to fuss far more over the criminal than they do over his victim.

Fraud is on the increase. Some years back villains were staging armed hold-ups, but today less and less cash is used so the things to steal are cheque books and credit cards. There was a man who even pretended to be ill and got himself into Guy's Hospital so that he could steal the doctors' credit cards. He and his gang then went all over the country passing dud cheques. When we caught them they said they had been enjoying their best holiday ever. There are much bigger frauds than that, though. I know of an outfit that had a bank in Bermuda, with branches in London and Geneva. Nothing could have been more respectable, on the surface, and a lot of their business was quite legal. However, from time to time, they pulled a really big swindle. It was almost impossible to spot because it took place in three stages in three countries.

Villains even take advantage of the Common Market. Many a commuter has left his car at the station, blissfully unaware that someone in Paris has placed an order for it! By the time he comes home, his car is in France. A few days later it has been changed to a left-hand drive and the satisfied customer has taken delivery of it.

Drug peddling is another thing that has increased, and this really is an international crime. The opium is grown in India, turned into heroin in Hong Kong and can come to Britain through America and France. A little bit of that is worth a lot of money. You can make a fortune from an amount you can hide in the spare tyre of a beaten up old car.

There is more and more violence, too. Did you know 8,000 policemen are attacked every year? You will have heard about soccer hooligans and National Front Demonstrations. Even quite reasonable processions will usually have a few extremists along with them, ready to make trouble. They spit all over us and roll marbles under the hooves of our horses, or stick hat pins into them. They are the same characters that turn up on the picket line during a strike. There is nothing the professional criminals like more than a good strike. They can burgle houses to their hearts' content while the police are busy keeping control at the factory gates.

It might be all worth while if the public showed us some appreciation, but they don't. I'm quite pleased to be retiring next year, as the job is getting more difficult all the time. We represent authority and today, more than ever, people don't like authority. You will remember those riots in the St. Paul's district of Bristol in 1980. Some said they were race riots, but white youths attacked the police as well as black ones. The trouble started because police officers were doing their job and trying to keep order. We shall have more troubles like that, believe me. Nor is it just the young who react against us. You wouldn't credit the abuse I have had from some apparently quite respectable motorists. Still, I know a station where they have the answer to that kind of person at least. They have put up a notice that reads, 'If you don't like the police, the next time you are in trouble send for a punk rocker'.

In some areas they are bringing back the bobbies on the beat, only now they are called 'community police'. Some of them walk around the district and some ride bicycles but the idea is the same. It is to improve the relationship between the public and the police. That in turn makes it easier for the police force to do its job properly.

There is a move back to this kind of policing, whether on foot or on a bike.

The prison officer

I became a prison officer because I hoped to do a bit of good in the world. I had heard about Prison Rule 1 which says, 'The purpose of the training and treatment of convicted prisoners shall be to encourage them to lead a good and useful life'. I'm afraid there isn't much chance of that happening.

There are the prison buildings for a start. Most of them are like the place where I work, well over a hundred years old. The huge gateway makes it look like a medieval castle, and you can imagine all sorts of cruelty going on inside. I suppose they made it like that to frighten evil-doers. It certainly frightens me.

The prisoners' day is hardly a good pattern for a better life. We get them up at six o'clock and the first thing they do is to 'slop out'. That means they all queue up to empty their chamber pots. The smell is dreadful. You don't often see the governor or the senior officers around at this time of day. Then they go back to their cells with jugs of cold water to wash, and we give each man a razor blade. We have to collect the blades again when they have shaved, of course. After breakfast they go to the workshops. Their main job used to be sewing mail bags, but that has finished now. Instead they do such things as tailoring and woodwork, but it is pretty dull none the less. The prison service itself buys most of the goods they make. No-one else would.

After lunch they have exercise. The exercise yard has three circular paths on it, and they just walk around them. Some of us are on duty, and we have dogs with us. The rest of the afternoon they spend working.

In the evening those that can be trusted are allowed some recreation. They talk, or play games like chess, darts and table tennis. There are even a couple of billiard tables. Some prisoners go to evening classes.

At nine o'clock we lock them up, and at ten o'clock we put their lights out. Patrolling officers go

Armley Jail, Leeds; built like a castle.

An officer supervising prisoners at drill.

Inside a prison cell.

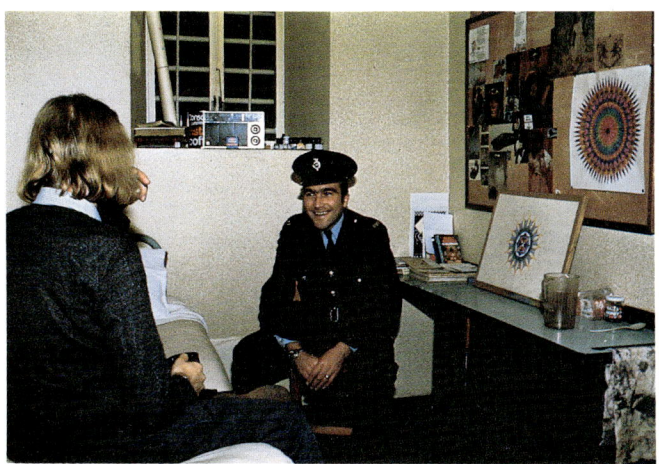

An officer chatting to a prisoner in his cell. This is what the officer in the story would like to spend more time doing.

round all night, looking through the peephole of every cell to see that its inmates are still there.

Food is very important to the prisoners and mealtimes are the high spots of the day. If there is trouble, a badly cooked meal is nearly always one of the reasons. If you ate prison food for one day, or even a week, you might not complain too much. It would be different if it was all you had for a few months, because it is deadly dull. Breakfast is porridge, a rasher of bacon, bread and margarine. Lunch will be something like shepherd's pie with cabbage, followed by suet pudding—all heavy and starchy. Tea is bread, jam and margarine. Most prisoners put on weight while they are in gaol.

The big problem is overcrowding. The cells were built to hold one man each. We have two in all of them, and three in some. I had to go into a cell the other night to take a prisoner some medicine. He was sitting up in bed, a clean young man with some photographs of his family on the wall. His cell mate was much older. He was lying in bed, smoking some foul tobacco. He was fully dressed and it was obvious he had not washed. He had a chamber pot beside him, half full, which he was using as an ash tray, and to spit into. The table was covered with sugar, bits of bread and spilt tea. The smell when I opened the door was so terrible I had to stagger back to take a few gulps of clean air.

One thing that nobody seems to be clear about is what a prison is actually for. Is it meant to reform people? I think prisons like this one only make people worse. Are they meant to protect society from dangerous criminals? That's a laugh. Most of our inmates are just petty thieves none of whom would hurt a fly. The judge called one of them a 'menace to society' when he passed sentence. The man had stolen 50p. His only problem was that he just couldn't give up stealing. You might as well be honest and say prisons are places of punishment, but who wants to spend his life doling out punishment? I certainly don't.

We uniformed prison officers have a raw deal. Not only are we badly paid, but there aren't enough of us. What is more, all the interesting jobs are done, and done very badly, by rather wet do-gooders. The worst here is our governor who is tough with his officers, and soft with the criminals. There are plenty of others, too, like the social workers and the teachers. Meanwhile, what is there for the officers to do? We count them, lock them up again, and that's about it.

Law and Order: Conclusion

In the eighteenth century police work was done by unpaid constables, and inefficient old watchmen. Prisons were, for the most part, insanitary dungeons, and no-one cared about the people in them. Today our police force is well organized, well equipped and, on the whole, efficient. There has been less progress in the prisons over the last hundred years, but at least the people responsible for them recognize that it is their duty to help the criminals lead better lives. Like the other human activities described in this book, the keeping of law and order has made a lot of progress. However, crime is also a human activity. That, too, has grown and flourished.

Questions

1. Why has crime increased in the twentieth century?
2. What new types of crime have appeared?
3. What problems do the police face?
4. How do men in prison spend their day?
5. What does a prison officer hope to do for the people in his care? Why is he likely to be frustrated?
6. What is the purpose of prisons today? Give three possible answers.

6 Medicine

Medicine in the Eighteenth Century

In the eighteenth century there were three kinds of doctor. There were physicians, who were like our family doctors, apothecaries, who were like our chemists, and barber-surgeons. The apothecaries and barber-surgeons were practical men who had learnt a little by trial and error. The physicians, who studied far longer than the others, gained little useful knowledge. They took their ideas from classical writers like Galen who lived in the second century A.D. They believed that the body contained four humours, that each of these humours gave the patient a particular kind of feeling, or temperament, and that each one was influenced by a heavenly body:

Humour	Temperament	Heavenly body
Blood	Sanguine	Jupiter
Phlegm	Phlegmatic	Moon
Yellow bile	Choleric	Mars
Black bile	Melancholic	Saturn

A quack at work. He is taking advantage of the belief that 'if it hurts it must be doing me good'.

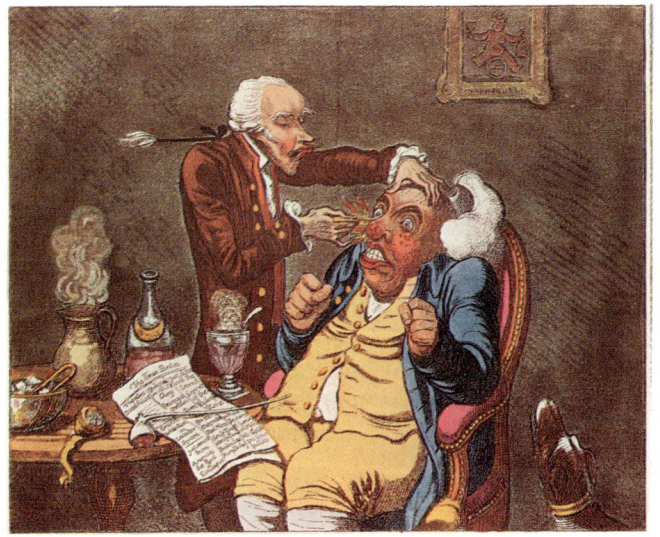

Pulling a tooth.

In the healthy body all four humours were in balance. In a diseased body they were out of balance, like a bad cake which has the right ingredients, but in the wrong quantities. The physician's job was to restore the balance. His usual cures were bleeding and purging, and he studied the stars to know when best to apply them.

Since doctors were not much help, many people went to 'white' witches and quacks. White witches used magic and strange medicines made from herbs and parts of animals. Some of these strange remedies actually worked, and the witches did believe in what they were doing. Quacks, though, were cheats, who just made up concoctions and sold them. A Joanna Stevens became famous for one of her mixtures, but it was made mainly of soap and snails.

During the eighteenth century, however, there was some progress. Surgeons separated themselves from barbers. They carefully studied the human body and they became very skilled at operations. They removed limbs and even gallstones, but having neither anaesthetics nor antiseptics they could not, for example, take out an appendix. Another branch of medicine which made good progress was obstetrics, which is about the problems of child birth. This was thanks, largely, to William Smellie. The most important discovery of all was when Edward Jenner found how to prevent smallpox.

A surgeon

As a surgeon, I think I can safely say that surgery is making more rapid strides than any other branch of medicine.

Not long ago, surgeons were thought of as being like barbers. After all a barber uses scissors and razors, which are the same tools the surgeon employs! I'm afraid it is still true that in the country areas people are still at the mercy of the barber-surgeons who will trim your beard, shave your head, bleed you, draw an aching tooth or cut off a shattered leg. In London, however, the United Company of Barbers and Surgeons has been dissolved and each has its own company.

Surgery is now making great progress. We owe much to William and John Hunter who came to us from the admirable School of Medicine that they have in Edinburgh. You will hardly believe this, but until they arrived all teaching in surgery was done by lectures. Now, students do their own dissections and learn in a practical way. Many of us are highly skilled. I am frequently worried before an operation and sometimes vomit at the thought of it, but once I begin I have complete control of myself, and more particularly, my hand. I can remove a gall stone from a bladder in thirty seconds, and amputate a limb in less than a minute. It is important to work quickly to limit the sufferings of the patient. Usually they welcome the operation, as anyone would whose limbs have been crushed, or who has suffered agony from gall stones for months on end. They have a strong dose of brandy before we begin, which gives them courage. Though they all sweat a great deal, it is rare for them to faint. No-one has ever died under my knife. It is after the operation that I begin to worry. Too many of our patients develop gangrene in their wounds and die from that. Whoever discovers a cure for gangrene will do a notable service to mankind, and surgery will be able to make even greater advances.

What is happening in other branches of medicine? Let us start with those who imagine themselves to be the aristocrats of the profession, the physicians. Why should they feel superior to surgeons? All that a physician has is a great fund of useless knowledge. He must study the works of classical authors such as Galen and Hippocrates, so he needs Latin and Greek. Because of the belief in the importance of heavenly bodies he has to study astrology. I am at a loss to understand what real use these things can be. Then he must qualify as a Doctor of Medicine at Oxford or Cambridge. For this he has to write a thesis, and pass an oral examination lasting four hours. The oral examination is in Latin! When you ask the reason for this, you are told it is to put students of all nationalities on an equal footing. I would like to know how many physicians have passed no examinations at all, but owe their positions to the favour of the king or some other great person. What I had to do was serve an apprenticeship and to qualify, pass an oral examination. This was in English and I wrote no thesis. That indeed may make me sound inferior to a physician, but at least all I learnt was of practical value. The physician has his head too high in the clouds. It is not even usual for him to visit his patient. The apothecary does that and then meets with the physician in some coffee house and describes the symptoms. The physician will then write out a prescription, which the apothecary makes up and administers. Only if the patient is very ill and very rich will the physician visit him.

As for the apothecaries, they are at least practical men, like the surgeons. They have a good working

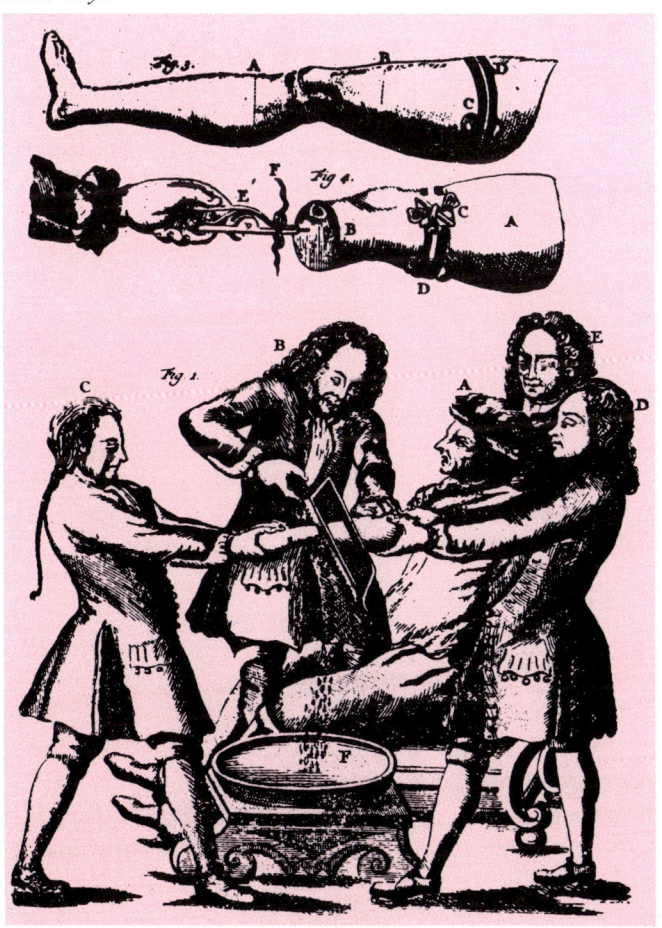

An amputation. Remember that there were no anaesthetics in those days.

knowledge of drugs and herbs, and are adopting others from abroad, like cinchona (quinine). I believe this is excellent for the ague. Sensible people send for the apothecary rather than the physician when they fall sick. Mostly, though, I feel that when the apothecary's concoctions cure a patient, this is due more to good fortune than skill.

A great problem remaining is that for many people, particularly the poor and ignorant, there is little difference between medicine and magic. A sovereign as recent as Queen Anne believed she could cure the King's Evil with the royal touch. It is still thought that the seventh son of a seventh son has magical healing powers. Country folk especially, prefer to go to a white witch than to any medical man. From what I hear of doctors in the rural areas, they may be wise in their choice! None the less, the eighteenth century has seen science make great progress at the expense of superstition. There is hope even for the physicians.

The smallpox

The disease which killed most people in the eighteenth century was almost certainly smallpox. It was particularly deadly to young children. A great many died from it and large numbers were blinded: even more were disfigured for life with the ugly 'pock marks' which were left after the sores had healed.

The first person to do anything about smallpox was not a doctor or a scientist, but a woman called Lady Mary Wortley Montagu. She was travelling in Turkey where she found that the disease, though very common, was also fairly harmless. This was because of inoculation which was done in the following way. A group of fifteen or sixteen children met together and an old woman came along with a nutshell full of pus taken from the sores of a patient suffering from a mild form of smallpox. She took a needle, made a scratch with it and put a tiny drop of pus in the wound. After about a week, the children were ill for two or three days, but according to Lady Mary, none ever died.

In 1721, after her return to England, Lady Mary persuaded George II to order the inoculation of six convicts in Newgate Prison, three men and three women. The experiment was a success, so before long many people wanted themselves and their families to be inoculated.

Inoculation must have saved many lives, but it did have disadvantages. In the first place, numbers of people did not have a mild attack of smallpox, but a serious one, from which they died. Further, even if they themselves escaped with a few days' illness, they were highly infectious, and could pass the disease in its virulent form to others. Inoculation could not conquer smallpox. Something better was needed, and it was discovered at the end of the eighteenth century by a Gloucestershire doctor called Edward Jenner. This is what he wrote about it:

'I was a pupil of John Hunter, a great teacher of medicine. I remember he said to me one day, "Don't think—try". I have since followed that advice.

Gloucestershire is a dairy county, where a great many cows are kept. From time to time a cow will become sick, one of the symptoms being unpleasant pustules on her udders. A dairy maid milking such a cow is likely to catch the disease herself. Her hands and arms will be covered with pustules like those on

King Charles II touching people to cure them of scrofula, a disease which they called the King's Evil.

The cartoonist, Gillray, is making fun of vaccination, but many people were probably scared of the new cure.

A statue of William Jenner vaccinating his own son.

the cow, she has pains in her limbs, she is sick, her head aches and she may even be delirious. We call this complaint "cow-pox". Certainly it is unpleasant, but no-one has ever died of it, and, what is even more remarkable, no-one who has had cow-pox ever catches smallpox. This is well known in Gloucestershire, but I took particular note of it myself. In 1795 I tried to inoculate Joseph Merrett, one of the Earl of Berkeley's gardeners, but nothing happened. He had already had cow-pox. I inoculated the rest of his family who all developed smallpox. Joseph remained among them, but did not catch the disease.

Remembering John Hunter's advice, I determined to try an experiment. I chose a healthy boy called James Phipps and in May 1796 I made two slight cuts on his arm. Into them I placed some pus taken from the sores of a dairymaid who had cow-pox. Within a week he was ill for a few days, showing all the symptoms of cow-pox, but he soon recovered. In July, I inoculated him with smallpox, but as with Joseph Merrett, nothing happened. I tried again several months later but he remained fit and well. I realized I had made an important discovery, one that could remove the most dreaded scourge of our time.

A slight problem was what to call my treatment, to distinguish it from inoculation. Finally I decided to call it "vaccination", "vacca" being Latin for cow.

Since that time I have vaccinated hundreds of people. They come to a little hut I have had built specially, near Berkeley Castle. I am pleased to say that many other doctors are now copying me, and are enjoying as much success. Is it too much to hope that one day there will be no more smallpox in the world?

I will admit that I am puzzled. Vaccination works—but why? How can an attack of cow-pox make a patient immune from smallpox? That is a great mystery, and I feel it must remain so.

Questions

1 What kinds of doctors were there in the eighteenth century?
2 What medical training was there?
3 What did people think was the reason for disease?
4 What progress was made in surgery?
5 Why was it important to prevent smallpox?
6 Explain 'inoculation' and 'vaccination'. How was each of them discovered?

Medicine in the Nineteenth Century

During the Middle Ages, and indeed long after, the disease people feared most was the Bubonic Plague, or Black Death. That vanished in the seventeenth century, though why it did so is a mystery. During the eighteenth century the disease that killed most people was smallpox. That was checked by inoculation and brought under control by vaccination. However, there were still plenty of diseases in the nineteenth century.

The one which killed most people was consumption, which destroys the lungs. Also quite common were typhoid, which is carried in drinking water, and typhus which is spread by lice. Both are dangerous and very unpleasant. The most dreaded, though, was cholera. This had been confined to the Far East, but because of improved communications it was able to spread round the world. There were several big epidemics between 1831 and 1867.

The new industrial towns were unhealthy. They had grown very quickly but without proper planning, sanitation or water supplies. Another problem was that still no-one understood the causes of diseases. Few doctors believed in the 'four humours' but instead they blamed miasmata, which were bad smells that poisoned the air. When there was a disaster like an outbreak of cholera, no-one knew what to do. They thought they should get rid of the filth that caused the miasmata, but by dumping it in the rivers, which were also the drinking water, they made things worse.

However, there was a lot of progress in the nineteenth century. Louis Pasteur proved that germs caused disease, and other scientists found the individual microbes and learnt how to deal with them. For example, the German, Robert Koch, discovered the germs of anthrax and cholera. It was then possible to develop vaccines against them. In surgery James Simpson found how to use chloroform as an anaesthetic. It meant that a patient could have an operation without pain. Later, Joseph Lister discovered that carbolic acid was an antiseptic, which meant it would kill microbes. Wounds no longer went septic so easily, and many more patients lived after their operations. Finally, the Victorians made a determined effort to clean their cities. Thanks partly to a civil servant called Edwin Chadwick, Parliament passed a Public Health Act in 1848. This made town councils provide proper

An operation where an early antiseptic, carbolic spray, and an early anaesthetic, chloroform are being used.

sewers and water supplies. Other improvements followed, such as the provision of parks, and the clearance of slums. Britain's cities, though far from perfect, were much healthier than they had been.

A town councillor talks about the cholera at Exeter in 1832

The news that the cholera was coming led the Corporation at Exeter to look closely at the town. We were horrified at what we found. The houses were overcrowded and insanitary: the courts and alleyways were piled with filth and there were pigsties everywhere. Much of Exeter was more like an ill-kept farmyard than a respectable city. The most serious problem was a shortage of water. There were many private wells, but their water was unfit for drinking. There was a conduit which never ceased flowing but people frequently had to wait their turn to fill their buckets. There was a water works, but it supplied only a fraction of the town, and during a drought could be out of action for weeks together. Most people bought their water from water carriers who collected it from the river, and sold it at a half-penny a bucket.

The Corporation appointed a Board of Health, which did all it could to cleanse the city. The piles of muck were cleared away, to the annoyance of many of the inhabitants who had collected them to sell as manure. The streets were thoroughly washed. The residents were ordered to keep their houses clean. The pigs were all driven out of the city. Hearing that flannel belts could prevent cholera, the Board of Health distributed 4,000 among the poor. All the

Cholera at Exeter; disinfecting the streets by burning barrels of tar.

Cholera at Exeter; an angry crowd follows the bearers as they carry a coffin underhand.

physicians volunteered to help the Board of Health and each was given a stock of drugs—opium, calomel, oil of peppermint, soda, mustard, turpentine and spirits of wine. A piece of burial ground in the parish of St. David was set aside for victims of the cholera.

In spite of the careful cleansing of the city, the cholera arrived in 1832, and spread rapidly. The Board of Health used large amonts of chloride of lime and tried what fumigation could do, by burning barrels of tar. The smell of the so-called disinfectants was worse than the smell of the cholera. Lime was supplied in great quantities. We placed piles of it in the streets, so that people who wished could take it to limewash their houses. Many of the back streets were white with it. The clothes of people who died of cholera were ordered to be burnt, and inspectors were appointed to see that this was done.

The first reaction of the poorer people was disbelief. They refused to accept that the cholera was among them, and would not obey the rules of the Board of Health on cleanliness. Later, they turned to drink, and bravado, making up bawdy songs about the disease. Finally, they gave way to fear and anger. The parishioners of St. David's were furious that their cemetery had been chosen for cholera victims. At the first funeral they attacked the grave digger, and broke his tools, so the Board of Health ordered the burial to take place in the Bartholomew Yard. To avoid infection, the bearers carried the coffin underhand, on straps, instead of on their shoulders. The crowd saw this as a mark of great disrespect. There was much excitement, swearing and abuse. People shouted that it was not a fit way to bury a dog. To prevent similar scenes, the Corporation decided to employ a hearse, but the mob was determined to vent its anger. As cholera victims were buried immediately, it was said that people were being buried alive. Undertakers were accused of making a fortune from the cholera. It was said that doctors were poisoning their patients so that they could have their bodies for dissection.

Fear, though, was generally stronger than anger. Much of the time the streets were silent, save for the tolling of the funeral bell. The only people in the streets were the doctors and their assistants, and the only carriage was the hearse.

So many died that extra men were needed to help with the funerals, but they demanded enormous wages, and would only stay at their work if given plenty of beer and brandy. They were then so drunk there was little they could do. Often, the scene at the burial ground was quite remarkable. Two men, their sleeves rolled up and smoking short pipes, carried the coffin from the hearse 'underhand'. The clergyman, in his surplice, stood so far away from the grave that he had to signal when it was time to lower the coffin. Quite often, the funeral was at night so it took place by the flickering light of one or two lanterns.

When the cholera finally left, the Corporation did its best to improve the city. We now have excellent drainage, and ample water gushing in all streets. There is a large cemetery, well outside the town, to replace the two overcrowded graveyards which are now closed and planted with trees. Over the grave of the last cholera victim we built a church as a memorial.

Edwin Chadwick and public health

The best way to deal with disease is to prevent it, rather than cure it. How much better it is to escape an attack of fever, than to recover from a long, painful illness! If we are to prevent disease, however, we must know what causes it. Most doctors now agree that it is due to miasmata. A miasma is a poison in the air, which shows itself by a bad smell. This, when breathed into the lungs, can cause illness, just as easily as when poisoned food or drink is taken into the stomach. Consider what happens if you put a bottle of prussic acid under the nose of an animal. The poor creature dies at once, because the miasma is highly concentrated. When it is diluted by fresh air the disease may take longer to develop, or it may be less severe. If it is diluted enough, there will be no disease at all. They have recognized the truth of this at the Bristol Infirmary where, instead of having their fever patients together in one ward, they have scattered them through all the wards.

To put it simply, then, to get rid of disease you must get rid of your bad smells. But what do we find if we visit the houses of the poor? Not only are they badly built, and overcrowded, but they are quite insanitary. Usually there is a common privy for an entire court of twenty or more houses. This is a brick-lined pit with a wooden seat. When the pit is full, the landlord is supposed to have it emptied. The men that do this task cause such a smell that they are only allowed to work at night. For that reason

Edwin Chadwick.

London nightmen.

they are called 'nightmen'. Far too often they are not sent for in time, so the privy overflows into the court. It may well find its way into the cellars of the houses. It is in these cellars that the poorest families live.

There are no underground sewers in our larger cities, except in the richer areas. Elsewhere there are 'kennels' which are open drains running down the middle of the streets. I have often seen children jumping in and out of kennels, splashing one another. Even the few sewers that exist are wrongly constructed. They are huge brick tunnels, large enough for a man to walk along. It would take as much water as you could find in a small river to scour them clean, but only a small trickle flows along them, so it is not long before they are blocked. Workmen then have to break into them to dig out the filth.

The refuse from the houses is kept until there is enough to sell to 'muck majors'. They then stack it in their yards, and farmers buy it for manure. There is one such heap in the heart of Greenock that must contain a hundred cubic yards of filth. The stench is terrible, and in summer, the houses all around swarm with flies.

Water is often in short supply. A court will have only one standpipe and though the water companies do not charge the poor, they only turn on the supply for an hour or two in the day. There is always a crowd at the standpipe then, and quite often fights break out. Nor is the water very pure. In London there are companies who pump their water from the River Thames, close to the outfall of sewers.

Is it surprising that every kind of disease is found among the poor, and that their houses are the breeding grounds of the cholera, which is a threat to us all? Yet the remedy is quite simple. It is not more doctors, more hospitals, more medicines. It is good drainage and a plentiful supply of pure water. Thanks to modern science we can have both these things. For sewers there are glazed earthenware pipes which can be laid quickly and easily. Moreover, they will never block as long as they have a good flow of water passing through them. I hear from Mr. Hawkesley that at Nottingham they have filter beds which purify the water of the River Trent, and enough reservoirs to meet all the needs of the town. Other towns could have the same. I look forward to the day when every house will have its own w.c. connected by drains to a sewer, and that greatest of luxuries, a constant supply of pure water. To be sure it will cost money, but I have worked out that it would be no more than a few pence on the weekly rent. It is only a fraction of what the working classes spend on drink and tobacco.

On the left, the Victorian water closet, considered a great luxury in its day. On the right, the Penstock Chamber for controlling the flow of sewage. The development of efficient sewage systems was one of the great advances of the Victorian period.

Questions

1 Why was disease a serious problem in the nineteenth century?
2 What progress was made in medical science?
3 How did the people of Exeter react to the cholera epidemic? Why were they unable to cope with it?
4 What did Edwin Chadwick think was the main cause of disease?
5 How did he think disease could be prevented? Why would many of his ideas have had good results?

Medicine in the Twentieth Century

During the present century, there have been great improvements. All the epidemic diseases that killed our ancestors have disappeared. For one thing, almost everyone lives under healthy conditions and for another, if someone were to develop say, typhoid fever, doctors would know exactly how to cure him and how to stop the disease spreading.

Scientists have found new drugs. One of the most important was penicillin, which Alexander Fleming discovered in 1928, and which Howard Florey first used successfully in the 1940s. Antiseptics can help keep a wound clean, but they will not kill germs which have invaded the human body, either through a cut, or any other way. Penicillin, however, will do this. After the outbreak of war, the Americans learnt how to produce it in large quantities and it saved many lives.

There have also been advances in surgery. An important event was Edward VII's operation for appendicitis in 1908. It seemed quite a daring piece of surgery in its day, but we think nothing of this operation now. Surgeons can perform what would have seemed like miracles only a short time ago. Heart transplants have attracted the most attention. They were pioneered by a South African, Dr. Christiaan Barnard in the 1960s. Barnard's patients all died after a while, but now it looks as if many of the problems have been solved and some heart transplant patients are living much longer.

While doctors and scientists have been making all this progress, the government has done its best to see that everyone has the benefit of it. Before the Second World War, many people dreaded being ill because they could not afford doctors' fees and hospital charges. Then in 1946, Parliament passed the National Health Service Act. There is a fund to which workers, employers and the government all contribute. It is used to pay doctors and dentists and to build and maintain our hospitals. As a result, anyone who is ill can be treated free of charge.

A Member of Parliament, 1948

I have been a Member of Parliament for the same constituency in a mining area of County Durham since the end of the First World War. I know from my work with them that the poor have two great

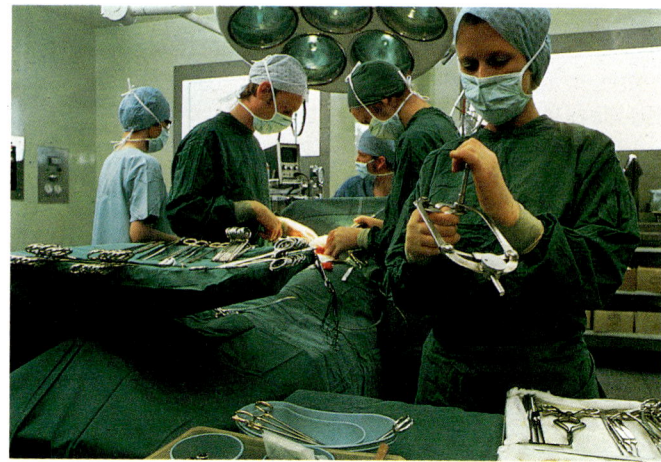

Inside a modern operating theatre.

fears. One is unemployment, and the other is illness. The two are linked because, of course, a sick man cannot work.

Unhappily it is the people who need medical care most, who can afford it least. You can see them in any street in my constituency, especially the miners with silicosis. They are fit only to shuffle about their homes or to sit at their front doors on a sunny day. It is the children who concern me most of all though. In the period between the wars many of them were a distressing sight. They were undernourished and had skin diseases like ringworm or bone complaints such as curvature of the spine. Bad teeth were particularly common, and I have known children of twelve or so with no teeth at all.

It is true that since 1908 we have had a school medical service of a kind, but the school doctors and dentists are too few. It is also true that the adult poor have always been able to have some help. There are doctors who run 'panels'. Their poor patients pay in a few pence a week, then have free treatment when they need it, and I never heard of any doctor who refused to treat patients simply because they had no money. Not unnaturally though, they give their best care to the rich. I was born into a poor family and as a boy I had to attend a place calling itself the Royal Infirmary. The doctors were rough and unkind, and as for the dentists, I can well remember the screams that came from their cubicles. I used to put up with toothache rather than go to one.

Hospitals are a big worry. Almost one third of them belong to local authorities—county councils and town councils. They range from the huge Victorian mental hospitals or 'lunatic asylums' to tiny little isolation hospitals, built when horrible

Medicine

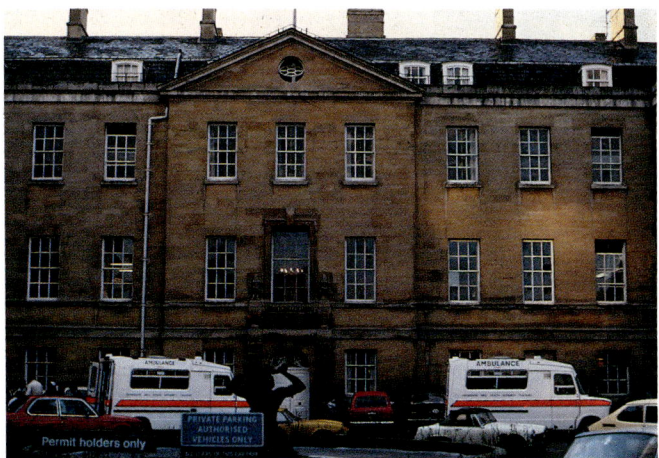

One of Britain's many old hospitals.

Bevan, the minister responsible, is 'treating' an opponent to his new National Health Service.

infectious diseases like typhus and typhoid were common. The other two thirds are 'voluntary' hospitals and these include the great London teaching hospitals like Guy's, but some are quite different. One I know was founded in the eighteenth century by a rich merchant. He paid for the building and then left some land so that its rent could be used for expenses. Today, charitable people give it contributions, it raises money at fetes and it has a number of wards for private patients who pay for their treatment. Without these fees, there would be no consultants, so the poor patients would have no specialist treatment. You can see that whether you have a good voluntary hospital in your area depends entirely on luck.

Doctors' surgeries vary greatly too. I know of one man who has put up a special building beside his house. It has a comfortable waiting room, a surgery with modern equipment and all spotlessly clean. He also pays a receptionist, out of his own pocket. He earns no more than another who sees his patients in his own front room, and yet another who has a primitive lock-up surgery jammed between a couple of factories.

None of this will do. Broadly speaking rich people can avoid catching unpleasant diseases, they can keep fit and active and they live for a long time. Surely, though, everyone has a right to these things, and now that the war is over we are going to see that they have them. To that end Parliament has just passed the National Health Service Act.

In the first place there will be no more local authority and voluntary hospitals. The government will take responsibility for them all. Of course it will bring the old-fashioned ones up to date and it will build new ones, wherever they are needed. The local authorities will still have plenty to do however. They will run the ambulance and home nursing services as well as dental clinics and health centres. They will also still have the most important task of keeping our surroundings healthy with sewers and supplies of clean water.

I'm afraid that doctors and dentists have not been too co-operative. They are very independent people and do not wish to be paid employees of the state. One of them told me that if he had wanted that he would have joined the Post Office. As the National Health Service cannot possibly work without the doctors and dentists, the government has promised them that if they join it they can keep their private patients. I must say I am unhappy about this because I think that medical care should depend on the patient's need and not on how much money he has.

People are already saying that the National Health Service will be too expensive. Well, you cannot repair the neglect of centuries without spending a good deal of money, that I agree. But what better investment can a nation make than in the health of its people? Also, I'm going to be rash enough to make two prophecies about the National Health Service. The first is that it is never going to take as much money as we spend on drink and tobacco. The second is that as it does its work, and fewer people are ill, then its cost will fall year by year.

The psychiatrist

I am a psychiatrist, which means I am a specialist who cares for people who are mentally ill.

Mental illness is becoming an even more serious problem than physical illness. There are all sorts of reasons for this. A lot of people have demanding jobs which involve stress. My own job is a good example of this. If someone like me is unable to forget his work, but takes his worries home and loses sleep over them, it is a clear sign he is heading for a breakdown. At the other end of the scale, there are people who have dull, boring jobs, perhaps in very noisy factories. Their jobs literally drive them mad. Also at risk are people who live in poor conditions. A man may live in a house that is so overcrowded he can never have a moment's peace, or a woman may have a family of young children in a high rise flat which is like a prison to her. Having nothing to do can be as bad as having too much. Many patients in mental hospitals are there because they were unemployed and became depressed. Sometimes, wealthy middle-class women can turn to drink and go mad with boredom when their children are grown up. We call this the 'empty-nest syndrome'.

A lot of people who are mentally sick are neurotics. They know quite well what is happening

A mental patient in a pottery class.

around them, but they cannot cope because they are too anxious, or depressed. A neurotic woman finds it too much of a strain to decide what to give her family for dinner.

A few patients are schizophrenic. They are truly insane for they have lost all touch with reality. The world, to them, is totally confused. Then there are the psychopaths. Their difficulty is that they cannot

Some examples of art by victims of mental illness. Art and pottery (above) are considered to be useful 'therapies' (cures).

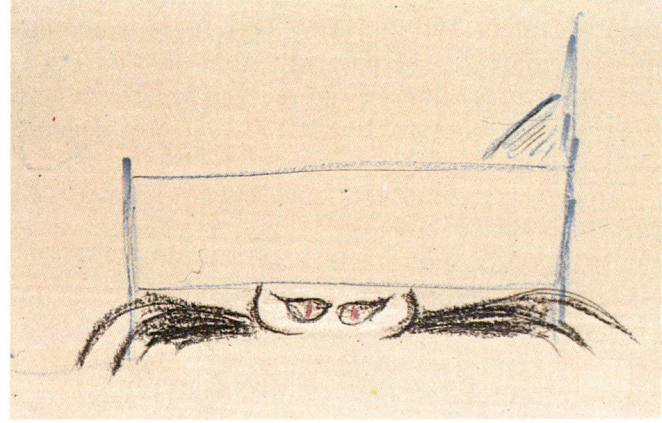

tell right from wrong. The worst psychopaths are very dangerous, for they will commit one murder after another, for no good reason, and with no feeling of guilt.

It will give you some idea of the problem of mental health when I tell you that of all the people in this country, one woman in six, and one man in nine, will spend some time in a psychiatric hospital. Many others will need treatment of some kind, even if it is only a dose of tranquillizers. Put another way, we have a quarter of a million people in hospital at the moment, and one and a half million out-patients.

To cope with all this mental illness there are only 835 consultants and there is a grave shortage of nurses. Of course we cannot possibly do all we should. The nurses try to help the patients by talking to them, encouraging them to talk to each other, and by giving them plenty to do. Mostly we rely on drugs. At least drugs will usually keep patients reasonably calm and easy to control.

Our buildings do not help. New hospitals are not for us. Mainly we have to make do with what were once nineteenth century lunatic asylums. The Victorians did not like being reminded about the insane, so they built asylums in leafy parks, well out of the cities. They are usually very large buildings with long, echoing corridors, and huge wards, big enough for fifty beds. All we can do to make the patients feel they are individuals is to give them bed-spreads of different colours.

I'm afraid the attitude of the public has not changed much for the better. When I tell people I am a psychiatrist, they usually look at me strangely, as if I were mad myself. Sometimes when I am having a converstation, a silly female will suddenly ask, 'Oh, Mr. Brown, are you busy psycho-analysing me?' I usually answer, 'Madam, you flatter yourself.'

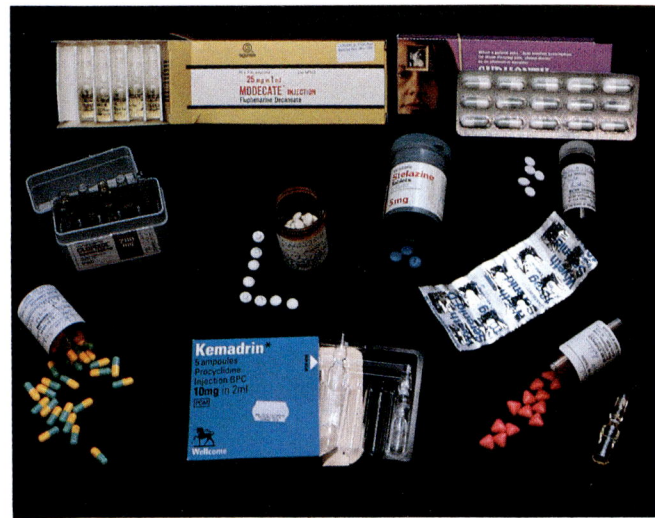

A selection of the drugs available for psychological problems.

young adults; today we die of cancer and heart attacks which are diseases of the middle aged and elderly. When we know how to deal with these, no doubt something new will appear that kills people who are older still.

Nor has the National Health Service been a complete success. As the last case study shows, it does not cope very well with the mentally sick. The elderly are, perhaps, an even more serious problem. Partly because of better medical care, more people are living into old age, so the number of old folk is increasing year by year. The National Health Service can hardly look after them all.

Also, even though we are, on the whole, healthier than our ancestors, there is no limit to the amount of medical care we demand. This is partly because patients expect a very high standard of care and treatment from their doctors, dentists and opticians. It is also partly due to the strains and pressures of modern life.

Medicine: Conclusion

There has been great progress in medicine over the last two hundred years, but as fast as the old problems have been solved, new ones have appeared.

The battle against disease is unending. In the eighteenth century people died of smallpox, which is a children's disease; in the nineteenth century they died of tuberculosis, which is a disease of youths and

Questions

1 What progress has been made in medicine in the twentieth century?
2 What was wrong with the medical services before 1946?
3 How did people hope the National Health Service Act would improve them?
4 Why is mental health a problem today? Why does the National Health Service have difficulty in coping with it?
5 Why is it likely that the cost of the National Health Service will go on increasing?

7 Inland Transport

Inland Transport in the Eighteenth Century

During the Middle Ages, and indeed, in the eighteenth century, most roads were only village tracks. Farmers used them to go out to their fields, with carts and animals, but apart from that, there was little other traffic. Since it was the villagers who used the roads it was only fair that they should look after them. That had always been the custom, but in 1563 Parliament made a new law, or statute, about the roads. It said that every year, all villagers had to give six days unpaid labour mending the roads. This was called 'statute labour'.

Statute labour was good enough to repair tracks, but some villages lay between important towns, and they carried quite a lot of through traffic. This increased a great deal during the eighteenth century. Farmers found they were mending roads, not just for themselves, but for people who had nothing to do with their village. It is not surprising that they did their statute labour in a half-hearted way, and that roads were bad as a result.

Another problem was that no-one knew how to make good roads. The Romans had been the last road builders in Britain. Later people did little more than fill the worst of the ruts and potholes with stones.

Though there were numbers of solid stage coaches and stage waggons in use by the early eighteenth century, the only way to travel at all quickly was on horseback. Goods also went by pack horse. The problem was the expense, especially for the goods. One horse could only carry about $2\frac{1}{2}$ hundred weight (125 kilogrammes). No-one could afford coal, for example, if he lived more than fifteen miles from a mine.

The only alternatives to roads were rivers. Barges were a cheap way of carrying bulky goods, but even so there were difficulties. Rivers can run dry in summer, and flood in winter, and unless there is a towpath, men have to pull the barges. A few rivers had been improved, like the Wey near London. In the 1650s Sir Richard Weston made towpaths along its banks and built locks to control the flow of water. He also dug cuts to avoid some of the larger loops in the river.

A coach journey in 1700

The coach left the Swan Inn in Piccadilly at five in the morning. There were six of us inside, an old woman sat in a huge basket behind the coach and several people clung to the roof, as best they could. The coach was a good, solid vehicle, but it was heavy and had no springs. It was as uncomfortable to ride in as a wheelbarrow. It was a frosty Autumn morning so those of us inside had a pile of straw to keep our feet warm. The people outside must have been very cold.

We rattled over the cobble stones of the London Streets, and that was bad enough. We were in real trouble as soon as we had left the city and were 'off the stones' as they say. Even close to London the roads have no proper surfaces, but look like badly ploughed fields. We saw lots of sheep and cattle on their way to Smithfield. Some of the cattle had walked all the way from the Highlands of Scotland, and others from North Wales. There were even geese from Norfolk. So that they would have some

Hogarth's view of a country coaching inn.

kind of shoes for the journey, their drovers had made them walk through a patch of tar, and then over a pile of gravel. There were also long lines of packhorses. Some carried hardware from the Midlands—things like locks, chains and cooking pots: others carried bales of woollen cloth from Yorkshire or East Anglia. All these animals churned up the road. Just once in a while we passed a stage waggon, hardly seeming to move, as its horses strained at their harness. There were also a few stage coaches like ours, bumping along at a walking pace. The day was fine, but a heavy storm of rain would have turned the road into a quagmire. That is why there were so few wheeled vehicles. There are none at all in winter. If you travel then, you have to go on horseback. Indeed, if you are in any sort of hurry, that is how you must travel in summer.

We saw the reason why the roads were so badly made when we came to a village. There was a broken old cart, loaded with stone, and a small group of men. Some were sitting on the grass, while a couple were shovelling in a half-hearted way, trying to fill the worst of the potholes with stones.

This poster advertises a four day coach journey to York (but it does add 'if God permits'!)

YORK Four Days Stage-Coach.

Begins on Friday the 12th of April. 1706.

ALL that are desirous to pass from *London* to *York*, or from *York* to *London*, or any other Place on that Road; Let them Repair to the *Black Swan* in *Holbourn* in *London*, and to the *Black Swan* in *Coney street* in *York*.

At both which Places, they may be received in a Stage Coach every *Monday*, *Wednesday* and *Friday*, which performs the whole Journey in Four Days, (if God permits,) And sets forth at Five in the Morning.

And returns from *York* to *Stamford* in two days, and from *Stamford* by *Huntington* to *London* in two days more. And the like Stages on their return.

Allowing each Passenger 14l. weight, and all above 3d. a Pound.

Performed By { Benjamin Kingman, Henry Harrison, Walter Bayne's

Also this gives Notice that Newcastle Stage Coach, sets out from *York*, every *Monday*, and *Friday*, and from *Newcastle* every *Monday* and *Friday*.

They were villagers doing their 'statute labour'—or rather, failing to do it. The only answer is to have the roads enormously wide. Those leading to London are 99 feet wide: between market towns they are 66 feet: even between villages they are 40 feet. That means a coach or a waggon has room to avoid the worst of the ruts and potholes.

As soon as we reached a hill, we all had to get out and walk. The coachman whipped the horses without mercy. At the end of the day, when they were tired, he beat them with a thing like a cat-o'-nine-tails. A coach horse is lucky if he lives for two years.

Our coachman was a big, rough fellow. I am sure he was drunk much of the time, but it did not seem to affect his driving. He said that the harness was always breaking, but he often mended it without stopping. Still holding the reins, he showed me how he could untie a knot with his teeth, and tie one with his tongue. He is certainly tough, and needs to be, or his coach would never finish its journey.

Bad roads were not the only reason why we took a long time. No-one was in a hurry. One of the passengers wanted to see a friend and the coach waited half an hour for him. Another had some business to do, so we waited for him too. We stopped for dinner and the innkeeper cooked us a good meal. After two hours or so, the coachman put his head round the door. 'The coach is ready, ladies and gentlemen' he said, 'But have another bottle of wine before you leave, by all means'. By the end of the day we had only reached Ware, just 25 miles from London. At this rate we shall be more than lucky to finish our journey to York in six days, as we were told we might, 'God willing'.

Questions

1. Why was 'statute labour' inefficient?
2. How were goods transported in the eighteenth century?
3. What problems were there with river transport? How were rivers improved?
4. Why was travel uncomfortable and slow in the eighteenth century?

Inland Transport in the Nineteenth Century

During the eighteenth century trade and industry grew so that there was more and more traffic.

Merchants and farmers were annoyed because the roads were so bad they could not send their goods to market at all easily. The government would do nothing, so people formed Turnpike Trusts. A Trust would have permission from Parliament to take over a stretch of road, usually about twelve miles or so. They would then put a toll gate at each end of it, and use the money to repair the road. Most Trusts employed skilled road engineers, two famous ones being Thomas Telford and John Macadam. There were hundreds of Trusts and by about 1830 they had, between them, improved all the main roads in Britain.

To carry heavy goods there were canals. The first of these to attract attention was the Bridgewater Canal, named after its owner, the Duke of Bridgewater. It joined Manchester to the Duke's coal mines at Worsley, eight miles away. After it was opened in 1761, the price of coal in Manchester fell by a half. It is not surprising that other towns wanted canals as well, and by the early nineteenth century, there were a great many.

While roads and canals were being built, a third form of transport was also growing. This was the railway. Since the sixteenth century owners of mines and quarries had built 'waggon ways'. These had wooden rails, and the trucks were drawn by horses. In the eighteenth century iron became plentiful and cheap, so owners of waggon ways protected their wooden rails by laying iron plates on them. Later, rails were made entirely of iron.

The iron waggon ways still used horses, but early in the nineteenth century two of James Watt's employees, Murdock and Trevithick built steam locomotives. Trevithick then had the idea of running a locomotive on rails. This he did in 1804. The early steam locomotives were not reliable, but gradually men like George Stephenson improved them. The next stage was to build railways, not just for mines and quarries but for the general public. One of these was the Stockton and Darlington. The first to use locomotives along its entire length was the Liverpool and Manchester which opened in 1830. It was a great success and soon much more ambitious lines were being built, like Brunel's G.W.R. By 1850 there was a network of 5,000 miles of track.

The Duke of Bridgewater.

A coach journey in 1830

I arrived at the Swan Inn just before five in the morning and bought my ticket. The coach was there, looking as handsome as a gentleman's carriage. Its varnish was shining, it had golden eagles on its doors, and its name, 'The Comet', in large gold letters on the boot. Its body rested on long curved springs, so it looked as if the journey was going to be comfortable.

Soon 'The Comet' was ready, and the passengers climbed on board. Four went inside, and the remainder, ten of us, went outside. I had paid £2.10s. for my ticket to York, which is as much as I can earn in a fortnight. To travel inside would have cost me £3.10s., which was far too much. The coach left at the right time, to the minute, and we rolled easily over the smooth London streets. On board were the driver, the guard, fourteen passengers with their luggage, many parcels, and three large trunks in the slides underneath the body. Even with all that weight, the horses went at a steady trot. There was a good deal of traffic, including many coaches. I am told that no less than 1,000 leave London every day.

Outside London, the roads were beautifully firm, with surfaces so smooth that there was no pebble on them larger than a marble. The horses kept on trotting and we covered the ten miles to Barnet in an hour. There we stopped at an inn. Ostlers were waiting at the roadside with four fresh horses which they exchanged for our tired ones in the twinkling of an eye. They worked carefully, but did not touch a strap or buckle twice. In just over a minute we were on our way again.

Over the next stage, the coachman did me a great honour. He let me ride beside him on his box. He was a smart young man, well dressed, and wearing a top hat. These days coach drivers are no longer the ruffians they used to be. This man was certainly an 'artist', as he liked to call himself. Now and then he cracked his whip over the horses' heads, but never once did he touch them. None the less he made them work all the way. We came to one particularly steep hill, and it was wonderful to see him take the coach down it. He held the horses in check until the coach began to press too hard on them. Then he 'sprung' them. A crack of the whip, and away they went, the coach bowling along at twenty miles an hour. It was half way up the next hill before the horses started pulling again. I asked him why he did not use his brakes, but he said only poor drivers ever did that. I also asked him what was the fastest he had ever driven, and he replied that he had once covered eight miles in twenty minutes. He had only two passengers at the time, and what was more, he was racing another coach. He said he would never do anything like it again. Three of his horses were so ill afterwards that they had to be destroyed.

Usually, drivers take good care of their horses. The animals are always hot and out of breath at the end of each stage, but it only takes them an hour to trot it, and when it is over they have finished for the day. The ostlers feed them well, and take much pride in grooming them. All the ones I saw were shining, sleek and healthy. With any luck a coach horse will live for six years.

At eleven o'clock we stopped for dinner, but the driver made it plain that we had only 25 minutes, and that anyone who was not ready would be left behind. The waiter served us a hurried meal, grumbling that the 'fast drags' were the ruin of the coaching inns.

I was already stiff by dinner time, and in the

'The Road-Side'. This picture shows one of the advanced coaches of the early nineteenth century.

afternoon it turned cold. Coaches run winter as well as summer these days, and I have heard of people freezing to death on them. By the time we reached Gainsborough, 150 miles from London I had had enough, and put up at an inn. I was glad to spend the night in a warm bed, rather than on top of the coach. I finished my journey to York the next day. The system is that the coach makes the whole journey, it changes horses every ten miles, drivers every thirty miles, and the passengers travel for as long as they can bear.

The Thames and Severn Canal

I'm the owner of a coal mine in Staffordshire, and I'm also one of the proprietors of the Thames and Severn Canal. That means I have shares in it. I inherited them from my father, and frankly, I wish he had placed his money elsewhere. I cannot sell the shares for they are almost worthless. The company hardly ever pays a dividend, and when it does, it is but a small one.

It is not that I blame my father. In his day, many canals were making excellent profits. He knew, moreover, that London was growing bigger all the time and needing more and more coal. The only way to take it to the capital was by ship, and the only coalfield near the sea is the one in Durham. The coal owners of the north-east had the people of London at their mercy, so they charged what they liked. But the midlands of England are rich in coal and the only problem is to transport it. If coal is carried by pack horse, it is too expensive to buy at more than fifteen miles from the pit, but it seemed that canals might be the answer. A single horse can tow a barge bearing the loads of 400 pack animals.

My father joined with other Staffordshire coal owners, and they in turn approached merchants in London. Together they formed the Thames and Severn Canal Company. At first the only worry was a pair of rival canals, the Oxford and the Coventry. They, too, were to join the midlands to the River Thames, and they had started work some years

The Thames and Severn Canal as part of the canal network and (inset) an example of the kind of barge still to be found on our canals.

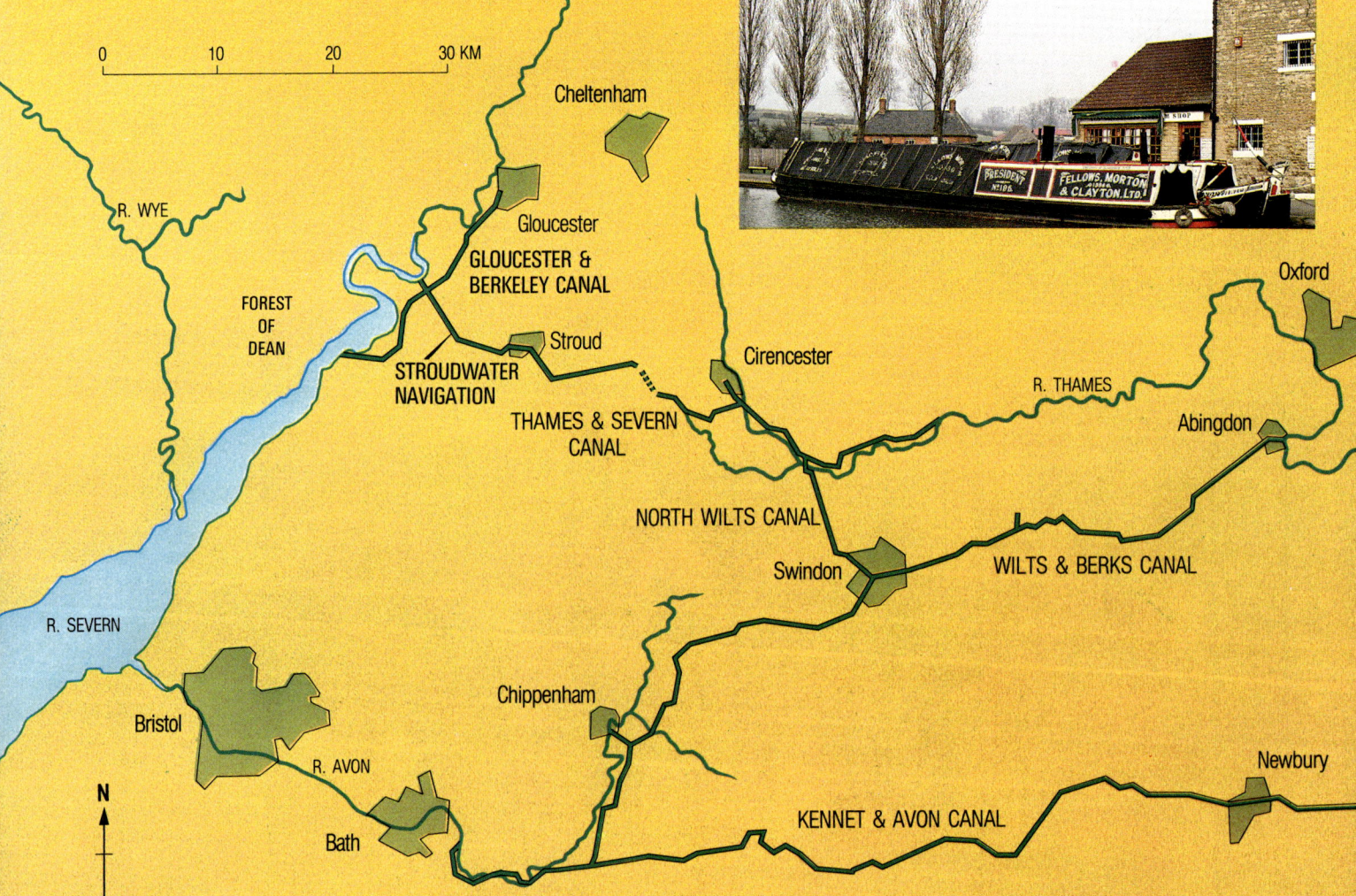

before. Nothing daunted, the Thames and Severn Canal Company set to with a will and finished their own canal before their rivals completed theirs. It opened in 1789, having been six years in the building. The proprietors sat back and waited confidently for a flow of traffic that would make them rich from its tolls.

That flow of traffic never came. After three years no more than four boats a week were sailing the full length of the canal. The merchants of Gloucester and Bristol still preferred to send their goods to London by sailing ships round Land's End and all the way up the English Channel. It was cheaper and quicker! As for goods coming from London, there were hardly any at all. The barges returned empty.

Looking back now, it is easy to see what went wrong. The canal was built for Thames barges. They are big, heavy vessels, shaped like punts, and ninety feet long with a beam of eight feet. At Brimscombe the canal joined the Stroudwater Navigation, which was built for Severn trows. Now a trow is usually seventy feet long with a beam of twenty feet.

Clearly, neither trow nor barge would fit a lock designed for the other. At Brimscombe, then, there had to be a canal basin and a warehouse where goods could be off-loaded.

Also, traffic by canal is slow. There are no less than forty-three locks on the Thames and Severn, while on the summit level there is the Sapperton Tunnel, two miles long. It has no tow path, so 'leggers' have to take the barges through. Moreover, the Thames has quite strong currents in its upper reaches, and eleven horses are needed to pull the barges up stream. Altogether it takes three weeks to do the return trip from Brimscombe to London.

Water itself is a great problem. The canal crosses the rocky ground of the Cotswolds. It has a lining of clay, but springs are always bursting through it, and when they subside the canal leaks. I have known it to be closed four months in the year because of loss of water, winter frosts and maintenance works.

One thing has been the saving of the canal. Recently the Forest of Dean coalfields have begun to prosper, and horse railways carry the coal to the

A Thames and Severn barge being pulled along by its crew. Horses were used on most sections of the canal.

banks of the Severn. From there, some of it finds its way up the Stroudwater Navigation and part of the way along the Thames and Severn. Even so, very little ever reaches the summit level. The dream was to send coal three hundred miles from the deep mines of Staffordshire to the great city of London. The reality has been to send it twenty miles from the Forest of Dean to the villages of the Stroud valley.

Henry Pease and the Stockton and Darlington Railway

It was my grandfather, Edward Pease, who should be thanked for the Stockton and Darlington Railway, and for all that it has done for South Durham.

In 1818, a woollen mill in Darlington burnt down, and many people were out of work. My grandfather, good Quaker that he was, wanted to help. He knew that industry would thrive in the valley of the Tees, if only there was an ample supply of coal. He also knew that there was plenty of coal around Bishop Auckland. The mines were ten miles from Darlington, though, so how could the coal be transported? My grandfather thought there should be a canal, but the country is too hilly for that, so it was decided, as a second best, to have a railway.

Few people in those days knew anything about railways, so my grandfather sent for George Stephenson who had built one at Killingworth Colliery. Stephenson thought the best idea was to take the line directly from Bishop Auckland to the sea, ignoring Darlington entirely. Old Edward would have none of that. 'George', he said, 'thou must think of Darlington. Thou must remember it was Darlington sent for thee.'

Another argument was about how to draw the waggons. The local men wanted horses, but Stephenson said they must have locomotives. He insisted that my grandfather and other members of the Company should visit Killingworth to see the ones he had made there. This time Stephenson had his way, or nearly so. The final plan was as follows. Horse drawn waggons were to bring the coal from all the different collieries to Bishop Auckland, while locomotives were to work the line from Stockton to Darlington. Between Bishop Auckland and Darlington there are hills which are too steep for horses or locomotives, so here stationary engines were used. We have built tunnels through the hills since then, but there was no money for that at first.

Another problem was the gauge. Stephenson solved that by taking the average of the colliery waggon ways in the area. He arrived at 4'8½". This is a strange figure you may think, but it has worked well. I understand that today almost all the railways in Britain use it.

The official opening of the line was on 27 September 1825. There was great excitement and much rejoicing. The first train was pulled by Stephenson's 'Locomotion' which we found could draw 75 tons at 5 m.p.h and quite cheaply too. It would have cost twice as much to have done the same work with horses.

The railway had its enemies, as you may imagine. When Lord Hartington found it was going to pass near his fox covers, he made so much trouble that we had to plan a different route for it. Plantation owners were worried, and I do not blame them. When our locomotives had no waggons to draw, the drivers used to run them at full speed, which was 12 m.p.h. They showered the pine trees with sparks, so we restricted them to 5 m.p.h. near plantations. Mostly the people in the Tees valley

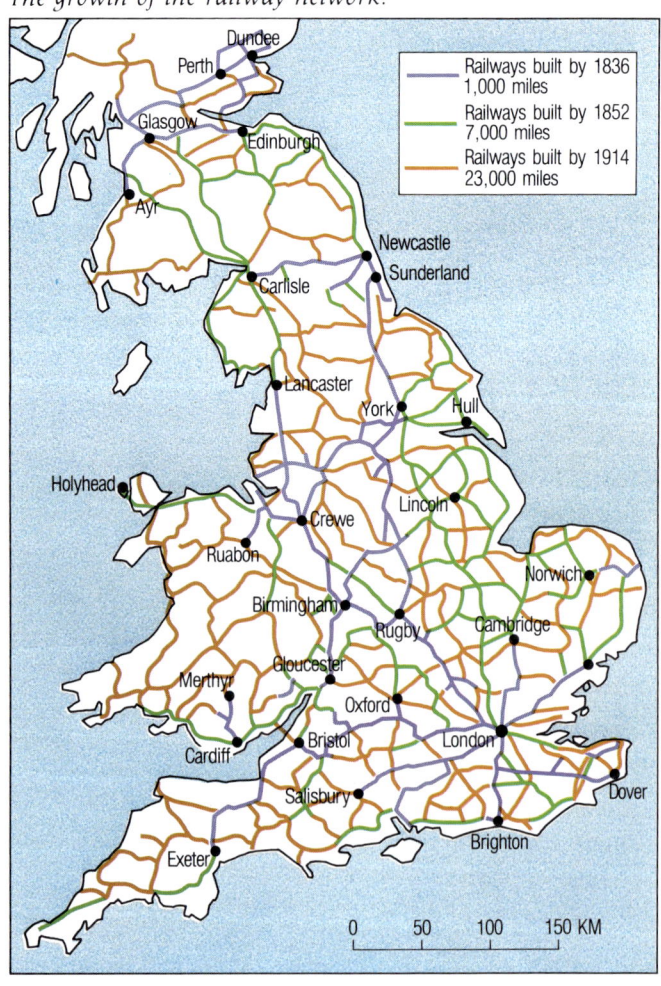

The growth of the railway network.

were grateful to the railway for all the cheap coal it brought them.

The original line was only twenty-five miles, but the Company now owns five times as much. We laid a railway into the Wear valley to bring limestone for the local farmers. So that we could export coal we went beyond Stockton and built the new port of Middlesbrough, 'Pease's port' they call it. As I know that workers need rest and recreation I extended the line to Saltburn-on-Sea, and built a fine hotel there.

Soon after 1850 something like a miracle happened. Huge deposits of iron ore were found in the Cleveland Hills. We at once built a branch line to Guisborough, and after that no town could have been better placed than Middlesbrough. It found itself connected by railway to unlimited sources of iron ore, coal and limestone. I believe it now makes more iron than any town in England.

I must add that other railway builders have not been idle. Railways have crept north from London and York, and south from Newcastle to join our own. My grandfather thought he was building a modest little line to take waggon loads of coal from Bishop Auckland to the valley of the Tees. It is now one of the busiest parts of a great national network.

Questions

1 Why were turnpike trusts needed? What did they do?
2 How had coach travel improved by the nineteenth century?
3 Why were canals built? What problems might a canal have?
4 How did railways develop before 1830? Why was 1830 such an important date in their history?
5 In what ways did the Stockton and Darlington Railway help the region through which it ran?
6 Why do you think the Stockton and Darlington Railway was such a success, while the Thames and Severn Canal was a comparative failure?

The opening of the Stockton to Darlington railway.

Inland Transport in the Twentieth Century

Modern motorway traffic.

After the building of the railways many canals and turnpike roads found themselves in difficulty. The railways were much better at carrying goods and passengers over long distances. Gradually the canals fell into decline. Horse drawn traffic did increase but most of it was local, just going to and from the railway stations. If it was possible to travel anywhere by rail, no-one thought of taking the coach. The road had become the servant of the railway.

Late in the nineteenth century, however, there were a number of important discoveries. One was the early 'safety bicycle', which replaced the penny farthing, another was the rubber pneumatic tyre, and yet another was the gas engine. The gas engine was the first 'internal combustion' engine, that is, one which burns its fuel inside itself instead of outside like a steam engine. Then in 1884, a German, Gottlieb Daimler, invented an engine that burnt patrol vapour rather than gas. Soon afterwards Karl Benz made a vehicle driven by one. This was the first motor car.

Fred and George Lanchester first built cars in Britain, but others soon followed, like Rolls and Royce. Several cycle firms started making cars.

As the early cars were hand-built, they were expensive, and only the rich could afford them. In 1909, though, Henry Ford began the mass production of his Model T. In England, William Morris and Herbert Austin copied him. The price of cars fell so that many ordinary families could afford them.

In 1892 Rudolph Diesel had invented another kind of internal combustion engine. This proved ideal for heavy vehicles, like buses and lorries.

The new vehicles caused chaos on the old roads built for stage coaches. Their rubber tyres made the dust and stones fly, and what was worse, there were many accidents. The government and the county councils decided to build proper motor roads. Surfaces were made of 'tar macadam', which is small stones mixed with tar. The roads themselves were widened and straightened.

Since the 1950s, the government has built a network of motorways. Today, it is the railways that are having difficulties. In the 1960s, the Chairman of British Rail, Dr. Beeching, decided to close many branch lines. Instead of 20,000 miles of track, Britain now has 13,000.

A lorry driver from South Wales

You might think that all lorry drivers are the same, but there are three quite different kinds—shunters, trunkers and trampers.

A shunter is a man who works locally. He will take out goods and deliver them, perhaps making several drops. He then goes to collect his last load of the day and brings the lorry back to the depot. A shunter will not travel great distances, and he spends at least half of his time loading and unloading.

A trunker drives long distances, following the same route every day. Usually he works at night. He picks up a lorry a shunter has loaded for him and drives it half way to its destination. Here he meets a trunker coming from the other direction. He changes his trailer for his mate's and then brings that back so the goods can be delivered by a shunter in the morning.

I'm a tramper. You know what a tramp is—he's a man who goes all over the place. So do I. I will tell you what I did last week which was fairly typical.

I began on Sunday morning and drove a load of steel to Birmingham. That was craned off first thing on Monday morning. I then picked up a load for Glasgow. The loading took four hours so by evening I had only reached Warrington. On Tuesday, I drove the rest of the way to Glasgow. My load was for several factories, so I needed all Wednesday morning to deliver it. I then picked up another load, one for Newcastle, but by the time it was on board it was evening, so I stayed the night in Glasgow. I left early on Thursday morning, and was able to make my delivery in Newcastle by mid-day. There I collected a load for Birmingham and I delivered that on Friday.

Saturday morning I loaded up some goods for Cardiff and managed to get home in the early afternoon, but only by doing a dodgy.

You can imagine how my wife hates my job. She is on her own most of the time. If a fuse blows or one of the kids is sick she has to cope by herself. She often says that I think more of my lorry than I do of her.

She worries a lot about the things she reads in the newspapers. It seems that lorry drivers are always being attacked by criminals who want to steal their loads. I must admit that I'm extra careful when I'm carrying cigarettes or treacle (whisky), but I have never been attacked and nor has any other driver I know. Then there are accidents. Well, I do agree that there is more risk of one of those, and lorry accidents can be really terrible. You sometimes hear of a juggernaut tipping over the side of a bridge into a river, or careering out of control down a hill, ending up in someone's front room. Still, a lorry is bigger than anything else on the roads, so if there is a collision it usually comes off best. I would be a lot more worried for my safety if I were a coalminer or a fisherman. My wife has gradually got used to the

A modern lorry; being loaded and on the road.

life and puts up with it because we need the money for the home. When the children are grown up, though, I shall become a shunter or give up driving altogether.

Meanwhile, I like my job. It's something you can take a pride in. When I'm driving in heavy traffic I have to make split second decisions the whole time. There are pedestrians everywhere and one of them could step off the pavement, without looking, at any moment. The roads are full of cars belonging to amateur drivers. Most of them don't know where they are going or what they are doing. I like taking my lorry through that lot, not only looking after myself, but making up for everyone else's stupidity as well.

Another thing is that I travel a lot. I have driven all over Britain, and most of the continent. It's new scenery and new faces all the time.

Perhaps what I like best is the freedom. As soon as I leave the depot with my lorry, I am like a captain on board his ship. There is no-one to tell me what to do. I start when I like, I finish when I like, and I stop for tea or a meal when I like. There are rules and regulations saying how far we should drive, and for how long, but it's easy to fiddle the log book. Don't ask me to have one of those tachometer things—a spy in the cab—that would take away half the pleasure I get from my job.

The railway enthusiast 1965

I have been interested in railways all my life, and I am most upset at what has happened to them over the years.

The great days of railway building were in the

The Sir Nigel Gresley, one of the fastest British locomotives ever. It exceeded 100 m.p.h. on many occasions and reached 112 m.p.h. in the 1960s, not long before steam locomotives were replaced by diesel.

nineteenth century of course, but the whole system was in good shape even as late as the 1930s. There were some splendid trains, like the 'Flying Scotsman' which ran from London to Edinburgh and the 'Pines Express' from Manchester and Birmingham to Bournemouth. I can remember the excitement when the 'Mallard' broke the speed record by travelling at 200 km.p.h. That record still stands. In those days railwaymen were proud, and it showed in many ways. Country station masters even used to compete with each other to see who could keep the best garden.

There was trouble brewing, even in those days, though. Road transport was improving the whole time, and people were using it more and more. It was unfair competition. The road haulage companies chose the goods that were easy to transport and charged less than the railways. Then they charged more than the railways for the goods that were difficult to transport. That way they carried just what they wanted, and the poor old railways had to take what they left. As for the bus companies, they cut their fares to one sixth of those charged by the railways.

Then came the war, and the railways played their part nobly. They carried millions of tons of materials to the munitions factories and took the finished weapons where they were needed. They also transported soldiers to the ports, especially when hundreds of thousands of British and American troops invaded France in 1944. Ordinary people were not grateful though. They forgot what the railways were doing to help bring victory. All they knew was that the trains were dirty and overcrowded, that they had no restaurant cars and that they often ran late. A very serious problem at that time was the lack of maintenance. There were neither the men nor the money to do all that was needed, and when the war ended the railways were almost worn out.

The years just after the war were terrible. For one thing, the railways were nationalized in 1947. This had to happen because the companies did not have the money to repair the damage done during the war. Lots of people didn't like the idea of nationalization. Instead of the good old L.M.S., G.W.R. and L.N.E.R. there was 'British Railways' and British Railways seemed to stand for dirt and inefficiency. Trains might set out from London, one after the other, and more or less on time. Then the front one might break down and all the others would have to wait until a relief engine came to its rescue. People should have blamed the war, but they blamed British Railways instead. What distressed me most was that railwaymen had lost their pride. Before the war every engine was gleaming. After the war a locomotive could run for years without anyone putting a rag to it.

Then, for a while, things began to look better. There were some splendid new locomotives, especially the 9 F's. There were 251 of them by 1960, and I would say they were the best ever built. All the time, though, road competition was growing. Petrol rationing ended soon after the war, and more and more passengers and freight went by road. The year 1959 was an ominous one for the railways. That was when the M1 motorway was opened.

The British Transport Commission tried to fight back. It decided British Railways must be modernized. They pinned all their hopes on the diesel locomotive. They said it was clean, fast, needed little maintenance and would start at once like a car, instead of having to wait to raise steam. But what is a railway without steam locomotives? It is like turning a man into a robot. That might make him more efficient at his job, but he has no soul, no character. Also, the way they made the change was madness. Instead of gradual replacement, they destroyed 18,000 steam locomotives in thirteen years, that is 18,000 pieces of the finest engineering the world has seen. They included a lot of brand new 9 F's with working lives of 30 or 40 years in them.

The latest disaster for the railways is Dr. Beeching. He became the Chairman of British Railways in 1962. Before that he had been a technical director of I.C.I. What would I.C.I. say, I wonder, if someone put a railwayman in charge of them? In 1963 he produced his famous report, and it came as a shock I can tell you. Out of 20,000 miles of track, 7,000 miles were to go, one third of the passenger services were to be withdrawn, and half of all our stations were to be closed. We called it the 'Beeching Axe'. Mainly it lopped off the little branch lines, and I agree they never made a profit. They kept many a country village alive, though, and how do you put a price on that?

Dr. Beeching changed the name 'British Railways' to 'British Rail'. He said it was snappier. I wonder if he really meant that by the time he had finished there would be only one railway line left!

Inland Transport: Conclusion

In the early eighteenth century many a person spent his entire life in his own village, without ever leaving it. Those who had to travel found it very slow and expensive. Moving goods was even more difficult than moving people.

Today, we can go wherever we wish, quickly and easily. We can buy goods in our local shops that may have been made anywhere in the British Isles, or brought in through any of our ports. What is more, the cost of transporting them will be only a tiny fraction of their price.

However, serious problems remain. In spite of Dr. Beeching's axe, and in spite of ever increasing fares, British Rail cannot make a profit. The country cannot manage without its railways, though, so the government has to make up their losses. In 1978, for example it gave British Rail a subsidy of £434 million.

In contrast, road transport does pay its way. Most haulage firms make profits and the government collects far more in taxes on vehicles and petrol than it spends on the roads. There are problems here, none the less. To realize what they are, all you have to do is go into a busy street.

Questions

1 Describe the development of motor transport in the early days. How have roads been improved?
2 Draw a map to show the journey followed by the lorry driver. What did he like and what did he dislike about his job?
3 Describe the decline of the railways since the 1930s. Explain why it has happened.
4 What has been done since the war to make the railways more efficient?
5 What regrets did the railway enthusiast have?

A disused railway station.

8 Sea and Air Transport

Sea Transport in the Eighteenth Century

Writing at the end of the eighteenth century, Adam Smith said, 'It requires only six or ten men to bring by water to London from Scotland, the same quantity of goods which would otherwise require fifty broad wheeled waggons, attended by a hundred men and drawn by four hundred horses'. It is not surprising, then, that as inland transport was so bad, a great many goods went by sea.

The most important cargo was coal. Though most of Britain's coal fields are inland the one in Durham is near the coast and has two good rivers flowing through it, the Tyne and the Wear. From here, collier brigs carried coal to many places along the coast, but most of all to London. Most towns and villages in the south took their fuel from their woods and commons. London could never have grown into a great city if it had burnt nothing but timber.

Though not nearly as important as the coastal trade, Britain's overseas trade was growing as well. Much of it was in re-exports. Colonies in America and the West Indies produced crops like sugar-cane and tobacco which would not grow in Europe. British ships brought these goods home, and then re-sold them at a large profit to other European countries. The usual way of paying for the sugar and tobacco was with slaves taken from the west coast of Africa, but the planters also wanted goods made in Britain, such as furniture, china and textiles.

Yet another trade was with the Far East, mainly India and China. The East India Company had a fleet of ships that brought back valuable cargoes of tea, silk, porcelain and furniture. East Indiamen were the finest merchant ships of their day, and as heavily armed as many warships.

During the eighteenth century ships were improved. They were built almost like floating shoe boxes so that they could carry as much cargo as possible. Their sails and rigging were also made less complicated so they could be handled by fewer men.

A full-rigged ship of the Atlantic trade.

One big problem was with ports. All the important ones were on river estuaries, so ships went up and down with the tide. That meant it was difficult to load and unload them. There were a few docks, but not nearly enough. Dock building did not begin on a large scale, even in London, until the nineteenth century.

The ship's captain

I am the captain of the 'Swallow', a full rigged ship of 300 tons. Our home port is Liverpool.

Three hundred tons is a good size for a ship in the Atlantic trade. It's not that shipbuilders couldn't make anything larger. The East India Company has ships of 500 tons, and I have heard of one of 1,000 tons. The problem with a vessel of that kind is filling her with cargo. We sometimes have to wait a while as it is.

I must say, though, that things have got better. I remember one terrible voyage in the Mediterranean, some thirty years ago when I was just a cabin boy. We started from London with a cargo for Lisbon and Leghorn. At Leghorn we found a small cargo for Palermo and then we went on in ballast to Jurgento. We took some grain from there to Lisbon and picked up a load of cocoa for Cadiz. We sailed nearly empty

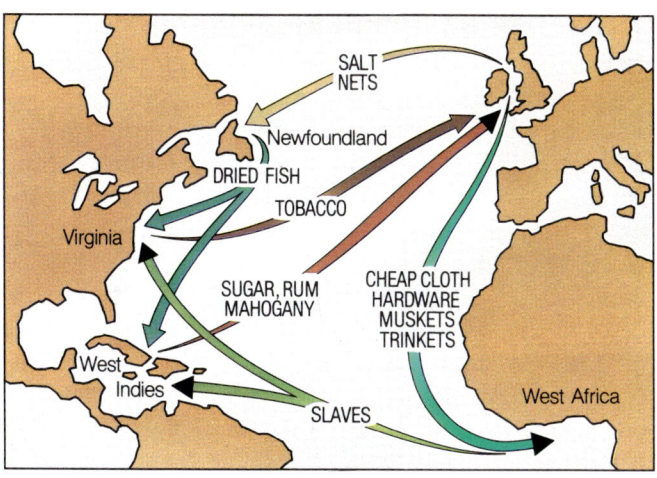

The two 'triangular trades' with North America and the West Indies. The more profitable was the one with slaves from West Africa.

to Genoa, but they had nothing to offer us there, so we went on, still in ballast to Leizat, in Sicily. Here we did find a full cargo of salt, which we took to Ostend, and from there we came home to London. For half of the voyage we had sailed almost empty or in ballast, and that is no way for a ship to make money.

Trade is now so good that we can stay on a regular run. What we do is take Cheshire salt out to Newfoundland. The folk there use it to cure their fish. We then take a cargo of fish down to Virginia where the planters want it as food for their slaves. In Virginia we lade tobacco, which we bring back to Liverpool.

The tobacco trade is much better organized than it used to be. When I was a young man, we would go to Virginia in October and then we had to tout for business all round Chesapeake Bay. If it was a poor crop, the planters had us at their mercy. If we wanted a cargo we had to fetch it ourselves. Many a time I have gone on shore with the rest of the crew and helped roll the big hogsheads of tobacco down to the ship. Some of those rolling roads are five miles long. Often, packing was not finished until the following June, and even then we might sail half empty. The Scots organize the business now. We don't go to Virginia until the spring, and we find the hogsheads all ready and waiting for us in the warehouses. We can be away again easily within a month.

Other ships from Liverpool also do a triangular run like ours, but their first stop is West Africa where they buy slaves. They sell these in the West Indies where they pick up sugar and rum, or in Virginia where they lade tobacco just as we do. My owners are Quakers, and so they won't have anything to do with the slave trade. Their scruples are costing them a lot of money.

I would not have you think that everything is easy. A lot could be done to improve our ports. Usually they are on river estuaries, where it is difficult for a sea-going ship to sail, and when we do anchor the tide drops us on the mud twice a day. If there is a port I detest, it is Bristol. First you have to sail up the Avon Gorge and when you arrive you have to cope with a tide that rises and falls fourteen feet. I was once lading in Bristol for more than three months, so my ship was dumped on the Avon mud two hundred times. It's a wonder she did not break her back.

Just once in a while we find a place in a dock. That's wonderful. We go in at high tide, the gates close behind us imprisoning the water, and the ship

Rolling tobacco barrels, Virginia.

A wreck on the Dorset coast.

then stays afloat and at the same level until we have discharged our cargo and laded another. I suppose there will be docks at every port one day: the sooner the better I say.

One thing that has not changed is the danger. Trinity House has some good lighthouses, like the new one at Eddystone. There are others, though, that are privately owned, such as Dungeness. Every ship that passes it has to pay a toll of a penny per ton of cargo when it unloads, so the owners must be making a fortune. But they don't play their part. Some nights the light is not even lit!

There are two kinds of sailor, deep sea and in-shore. They say the in-shore sailor is terrified if he cannot see the land, while the deep-sea sailor is terrified if he can. Well, I am a deep-sea sailor and there is nothing I hate more than being in the dark, hearing the boom of surf on a reef, and not knowing just where it may be.

A captain of a collier brig

I am the captain of a collier brig. She is a good, stout, seaworthy vessel, and I'm sure she could sail round the world if she had to. She has only two masts as you can see. Some years ago every vessel much above 60 tons had three masts, but now we have two-masters as large as 150 tons. I can run this brig with a crew of six, but if I had a three-masted ship the same size I should need a crew of ten. There would be so many more sails to handle. The smaller crew pleases my owners, because there are less wages to pay. Having fewer sails pleases me, because the vessel is easier to handle. You can imagine what it is like trying to beat up a river estuary against a head wind. There is no room to go about, so we do one leg of the tack, and then let the wind blow us backwards to the other side of the river. We make a bit of way, as long as the tide is running strongly in our favour. It is a tricky thing to do, and the fewer sails we have the better.

I have visited every port and harbour on the east coast of England, and sailed up every river deep enough to take my brig. I have been along the south coast, too, as far as Poole and Lyme Regis in Dorset. Beyond that we don't go, for we meet colliers coming from South Wales. Being nearer home they can undersell us anywhere in Devon and Cornwall.

Buying and selling the coal is my responsibility. To please my owners I must pay little for it, and sell it dear. That is not easy when trade is bad. The measure we use is the Newcastle chaldron. Some of the mines are ten or twelve miles from the Tyne, so their owners have built wooden railways worked by horses. The waggons they draw are called chaldrons. Each holds about seventeen hundredweight.

Loading the brig is the duty of the keelmen. Their vessels, or keels, are very ugly. Each is about forty feet long, twenty feet wide and is pointed at both ends. It will hold about twenty chaldrons. Its crewmen propel it as well as they can with poles and oars, but usually they wait for the tide. Keels are filled easily enough, for each chaldron simply

A collier brig, moored in the Thames.

tips its load down a chute. When the coal reaches the brig though, the keelmen have to cast it on board with shovels. If the brig is empty and high in the water, they may have to throw it eight feet. They object strongly.

Once we reach London, it is my crew that has to discharge the cargo. We erect staging in the hold and the men throw the coal from one level to the next, until it reaches the deck. Here it goes into a vat so that it can be measured ready to be taxed.

Sailing round the coasts of Britain is a tricky business, and many good vessels are wrecked every year. Also, there is now such a demand for Newcastle coal that we sail in winter as well as summer, so we are even more at risk.

There are few trades as important as the coal trade. In the Thames we are scorned by the crews of the East Indiamen. These are fine vessels indeed, armed like men of war and they sail all the way to India and China. We only have a dirty little brig, her sails grimy with coal dust and we don't sail farther than Newcastle. I can tell you this, though. If the trade with the East ended, we could manage well enough without its tea, spices, fancy silks and porcelains. If the coal trade ended, London would freeze to death in a single winter. Villagers can look for firing on the common, but what could the people of London do? It is Newcastle coal which keeps the capital alive, and it is collier brigs like this one which deliver it. How else could it come? London consumes half a million tons a year and there are not enough packhorses and waggons in the whole of Britain to carry that amount.

There is another reason why the nation should be grateful for the coal trade. A seaman can have no better schooling than the one he receives on a ship like this. What happens in time of war? The Royal Navy suddenly needs thousands of sailors and there are none which the pressgang seeks more eagerly than the crews of collier brigs.

Questions

1 What goods did Great Britain import in the eighteenth century?
2 Draw maps to show the voyages made by the ship's captain, and also the routes followed by ships engaged in the slave trade. Indicate the goods carried on the two 'triangular trades'.
3 What improvements had the captain seen in his lifetime? What others did he hope to see?
4 Why was the coal trade important? What dangers and difficulties did the sailors face? Draw a map to show where coal was mined and where it was sold.

An East Indiaman. Notice the many guns.

Sea Transport in the Nineteenth Century

During the nineteenth century many improvements were made to sailing ships. The most famous were the clippers. They were designed for speed, so they had fine lines and huge areas of sail. For the tea trade with China, this was ideal, though on many routes they would not have been a lot of use because they were not the shoe-box shape and so could not carry much cargo for their size.

While sailing ships were reaching perfection, a rival was on its way—the steam ship. One of the first was William Symington's 'Charlotte Dundas' which steamed twenty miles up the Forth-Clyde Canal in 1802. The earliest steamers did not dare go to sea, but they were ideal for river estuaries. Here, sailing ships found it hard to manoeuvre, but there were no tow paths for horses to pull barges. Then, in 1815, the 'Thames' steamer went from Glasgow to London in sixteen days. Before long there were hundreds of little steamers plying round the coast as well as crossing to Ireland and France. Until the railways were finished, they carried thousands of passengers every year.

The man who built the first ocean-going steamers was Isambard Kingdom Brunel. He designed three—the 'Great Western' of 1,340 tons, launched in 1838, the 'Great Britain' of 3,400 tons, launched in 1843, and the 'Great Eastern', of 19,000 tons, launched in 1857. Brunel was not very successful, mainly for two reasons. The first was that he had to use iron, and in order to be strong enough, the metal had to be thick. The ships were heavy for their size. Next, steam engines were not powerful, and they burnt a great deal of coal.

Later, men like Henry Bessemer discovered how to make cheap steel. Steel is much stronger than iron, so less of it was needed. Also, the steam engine was improved, so that it was more powerful and burnt less fuel. Every ton of metal saved on the hull, and every ton of fuel saved by the engines meant extra cargo. By the end of the nineteenth century steamships were efficient and sailing ships were rapidly going out of use.

The steamship Leith, *1841. She is later than the* Victoria *and, at 1000 tons, a good deal larger.*

The steamer captain

I am the captain of the steamer 'Victoria'. She is one of the latest design, being 150 tons, which is a good size, and having a composite hull. That means she has iron ribs, though her planking is of wood. No doubt steamers will one day be made entirely of iron, and they will be a good deal safer. Our engines have not let us down yet, but we carry sails in case they ever should. We hoist the sails, too, if the wind is right. They help us make a few extra knots.

To my mind, the development of the steam ship is one of the most important things that has happened in recent years. They carry thousands of passengers round the coasts of Britain every year, and at a fraction of the charges made by the stage coaches. Besides, there are not enough coaches for them all. Also, we go across to Ireland, so of course, it is sailing ships rather than stage coaches which we are putting out of business on that run. It has not been difficult to do. You can have no idea how hard it is to handle a sailing ship in a river estuary. A steamer just goes straight to her landing stage. More important, is that a steamer is faster and much more reliable. On a reasonable day we can reach Dublin fourteen hours after leaving Liverpool. No sailing ship could match that, and if the winds were contrary, the voyage might take a week.

The only problem is that too many people have seen the value of steamers. As well as Langtrys, my own firm, there are a number of steam packet companies, like the British and Irish, the St. George, the Dublin, the Belfast and the Coast Lines, and many more. They are all in competition with each other, and at one time charges were so low it was impossible to make a profit. The fare to Ireland was only 3d, and that included the price of a meal. In the end, the companies got together and shared the business between them. It was the only way to avoid going bankrupt.

Trade with Ireland is growing the whole time. Liverpool is a big place, while further inland is Manchester, and all the cotton manufacturing towns of Lancashire. The people there need food, so we bring it to them from Ireland, grain, butter, cheese, bacon and meat. Sometimes we carry live cattle, which is meat as fresh as you can have it. In return we take cotton goods, Lancashire coal and Cheshire salt back to the Irish.

One of our most important cargoes is people, especially in the spring and autumn. A great many of the peasants in the west of Ireland have farms that are too small to give them a living. When they have planted their potatoes they tramp all the way across the country and take ship at Belfast, Dublin or Cork. They work all summer in England, helping first with the haymaking and then with the corn harvest. Each will hope to save £10 or so from his wages, enough at any rate to pay the rent of his farm. They then go home and idle away the winter in their mud cabins.

I have had more than two hundred Irish men on board at a time, clad in rags, with their thin coats held together with wisps of straw, sea-sick and shivering with the cold. Sometimes when I have had no cargo, I have taken them free of charge. I would as soon have ballast that can walk on board and then walk off again, as sand and earth which have to be shovelled.

Steamers have done so well in the past that I wonder what future they have. I have been told railways will put them out of business. I can see the day coming when a passenger from Edinburgh to London will prefer to go by train, but they cannot build railways across the Irish Sea. Things work out very well for us. We carry goods between England and Ireland and the railway carries them between Liverpool and Manchester. We work in partnership, not in competition. I think the more railways there are, the more steamships will be needed to keep them busy.

'The Emigrants' by E Nicol.

Will steamships ever put sailing ships out of business on the oceans of the world, as they have done on the Irish Sea? That is a difficult question. I have no doubt that the 'Victoria' could cross the Atlantic, but I made an interesting calculation the other day. If she used her engines all the way to New York, she would have to carry so much coal there would be no room for cargo or for passengers.

A steam ship engineer

I used to be an engineer on board the 'Great Eastern'. That ship was to have been the wonder of the age: in the end she was one of its biggest disasters.

When I was a small boy a steam engine was a rare sight. It was all windmills and watermills for power, and when we travelled, which wasn't often, we went by stage coach. By 1850, however, it seemed as if the age of steam had arrived. The bigger, more go-ahead factories had steam engines, the country had about 5,000 miles of steam railways, while steam ships swarmed all round the coasts and crossed regularly to France and Ireland. The big question now was whether steam could conquer the oceans of the world. One man at least, Mr. Brunel, was sure it could.

The big problem with the older steam engines was that they burnt a lot of fuel. A steam ship going on a long voyage needed so much coal she could not take any cargo. Mr. Brunel realized that you could take advantage of what we call 'economies of scale'. If you make a ship four times as big as another, she only needs twice as much fuel. The larger you make her, the less fuel she burns for every ton of her weight. Mr. Brunel proved that when his 'Great Western' raced the 'Sirius' to New York in 1838. We know the 'Sirius' won by a few hours but only because she left four days earlier. The important thing was that the 'Sirius' burnt every scrap of her coal, whereas when the 'Great Western' arrived she still had enough for another 1,000 miles steaming.

Brunel's 'Great Britain' being refitted for exhibition in Bristol.

This was because the 'Great Western' was 1,340 tons, twice the size of her rival. The 'Sirius' was soon back on the Irish Sea where she belonged, but the 'Great Western' went on crossing the Atlantic, and so did Brunel's next ship, the 'Great Britain'.

Then in 1851 they discovered gold in Australia, and people couldn't wait to get out there. The best sailing ship took three months, and it might be weeks longer than that. You were never sure with sail, so folk wanted to travel by steam. Australia is nearly 12,000 miles away, and that is four times the distance across the Atlantic. The Eastern Steam Navigation Company asked Brunel what could be done, and his answer must have taken their breath away at first. He said he would build a ship 700 feet long and weighing 19,000 tons. She would be six times as large as anything afloat. The Company decided to go ahead, and asked Brunel to be their engineer. It was to be a tragedy for both of them.

Isambard Kingdom Brunel.

Mind you, the 'Great Eastern' had her good points. She was so large she could keep steady even in rough seas. She had a double hull, and was divided into twelve watertight compartments, so I don't think she would ever have sunk. Once, near New York, a reef tore a large hole in her outer skin. Most of the passengers did not even realize anything was wrong.

In spite of her good points, bad luck seemed to dog her all the way I'm afraid. Her launching in 1857 was a fiasco. Half of London must have been there to watch, and you can imagine what the crowds said about Brunel when, at the end of the day, the ship had barely moved. It took weeks to get her afloat, edging her down the slipway inch by inch. There were money troubles as well. Brunel thought at first she might cost £500,000. Her builder Scott Russell thought she could be made for less than £400,000. In the end she cost over £1 million. Russell went bankrupt, and so did the two companies that owned her. The biggest disaster of all was on her maiden voyage in 1859. Someone left a stop cock shut by mistake, and there was an explosion that wrecked her saloon, blew off one of her funnels and killed five of her crew.

The problems weren't all caused by bad luck. There was no steam engine made in the 1850s that could raise enough power for a ship of that size. The 'Great Eastern' was supposed to do 20 knots, but she rarely managed 14. We have compound engines now, that give much more power for less fuel. Another thing was that the ship was built entirely of iron which made her terribly heavy for her size. Today we use steel which is much stronger than iron, so less is needed. A ship of the same size as the 'Great Eastern' would be much lighter today. I am sure it will not be long before someone builds another like her, and she will be a success. Brunel's mistake was to attempt too much, too soon. His fine ship is now tied up at Liverpool, being used by a fun fair.

Questions

1 How were clippers different from other sailing ships?
2 How did the steam ship develop?
3 Why were the coastal and cross channel steamers important?
4 Why were the first steamers not suitable for ocean voyages?
5 What made Brunel think ocean-going steamers could be a success? Which of his ships proved him right? Why was his *Great Eastern* a failure?

Air Transport in the Twentieth Century

In 1897 Sir Charles Parsons produced the most efficient steam engine ever made. This was the steam turbine. It could power ships of over 80,000 tons, so, in the first part of the twentieth century many great liners were built. They included Germany's 'Deutschland', France's 'Normandie', and Britain's 'Queen Mary'. With their restaurants, shops, swimming pools and bars, they were like floating towns. They carried passengers all over the world, but most of them across the Atlantic.

While the steamship was reaching its peak, air transport was developing. In 1903 two American brothers, Wilbur and Orville Wright, made the first aeroplane flight. At about the same time a German, Count von Zeppelin, was building airships. In those days it seemed that the airship would be the better of the two. It could carry its passengers in almost as much comfort as an ocean liner. Also, it appeared to be safer than an aeroplane, because if its engines

Early air travel; the Zeppelin (below) and a poster for Imperial Airways, now British Airways (right).

failed it did not crash. In fact, airships were dangerous because the gas they used was hydrogen, and the smallest spark would make it explode. After the 'Hindenburg' caught fire in 1937, no more airships were built. They would probably have gone out of use anyway, because they travelled at only 40 m.p.h.

Meanwhile, the aeroplane was developing rapidly. In 1909, Louis Bleriot flew the English Channel. Then came the First World War, and aeroplanes proved so valuable that great progress was made in their design. By the time the war ended in 1918, the British had bombers that could have flown to Berlin. They could also cross the Atlantic, as Alcock and Brown proved, when in 1919 they flew a Vickers 'Vimy' from Newfoundland to Ireland. There were other pioneer flights, like that of Charles Lindbergh who, in 1927, flew on his own from New York to Paris. Companies such as British Airways and Imperial Airways began to run regular passenger services.

The Second World War saw many new

developments, including Sir Frank Whittle's invention of the jet engine. Since the war ended most passengers have chosen to travel by jet aircraft instead of by ocean liner.

In the 1960s it was not clear how the aeroplane should develop. Should it be made to go faster, or should it be made larger to carry more passengers? The French and the British decided on speed, and built 'Concorde'. The Americans chose size and built 'jumbo jets'. At the moment, it looks as if the Americans were right.

An aeronautical engineer, 1969

Concorde is one of the greatest scientific achievements of all time, but I think nothing has ever attracted quite as much stupid and unfair criticism.

People grumble about the cost. In 1959 the Supersonic Transport Aircraft Committee estimated that £90 million would be needed to develop Concorde. That included designing it, doing all the research and building a couple of full sized trial models. By 1966 it looked as if the figure would be £500 million and now we expect it to be £800 million. On top of that £300 million will have to be spent on factories to make aircraft to sell. This is a lot of money, but spread over the years it will only come to about one penny of every £4 you pay in taxes. When we think of it like that it does not seem too much. Besides, who can say what benefits will come from building Concorde? We now know far more about such things as electronic computers, fuel systems, radar, metals, tyres and so on. Scientists and engineers will use this knowledge in other industries and you may well have a better washing machine or a safer motor car because of Concorde.

Will people wish to take advantage of faster travel? Well, we have the experience of the jet aircraft. When it was introduced it increased the speed of flight from 400 m.p.h. to 600 m.p.h. in one jump. Not only did everyone at once wish to travel by jet, but the number of passengers travelling by air rapidly increased. Now Concorde will halve the time taken by the fastest jet. Would you take twice as long as you need over a journey?

Design problems have been tough. Flying conditions are quite different when you are going faster than the speed of sound. A subsonic aircraft sends its noise ahead of it, and the air divides neatly in front of its wings. It is rather like a crowd dividing for a motorist who sounds his horn. A supersonic aircraft, though goes faster than its own noise. It is

The Concorde airliner.

as if the air has no warning it is coming, and the aircraft forces it out of the way, setting up shock waves. The swept back wing is the best shape for supersonic flight which is why Concorde has delta wings. They are not much use for subsonic flight. At lower speeds they don't give enough lift, so the aircraft needs a lot of fuel.

If it is to be economical, Concorde must fly at the speed for which it is designed, over twice the speed of sound. However, when it does that, we run into another problem. The shock waves I told you about cause sonic boom. You might ask why the aircraft can't slow down overland, just as a car does in a built-up area. The trouble is that acceleration uses an enormous amount of fuel. On a flight to the United States, Concorde will use a third of its fuel just reaching its cruising speed of 1,400 m.p.h. If it did that twice, it would not have enough fuel to finish its journey.

One answer would be to fly Concorde only over the seas, deserts and jungles, which after all, cover most of the globe. It would be better, surely, to educate the public to put up with the sonic boom, just as they do with the noise of cars, trains and transistors. I agree strange things have happened. A French farmhouse was hit by sonic boom, and eight tons of barley fell through the ceiling, killing three people. How many of us, though, keep eight tons of barley in our bedrooms? Fighter aircraft have been making sonic booms for years, and as far as I can see the only buildings to suffer were those that needed repair anyway. As for the effect on people, I haven't heard of any surgeons letting their knives slip, or of any window cleaners falling off their ladders. Folk that are against Concorde are like the ones that said trains travelling at 30 m.p.h. would ruin our health, and insisted that a man with a red flag should walk in front of every motor car. When Concorde is flying it will be possible to travel anywhere in the world in twelve hours. Going to America will take only $3\frac{1}{2}$ hours instead of 7. Flying west, the traveller will go faster than the sun, so if he leaves London at 10.00 a.m. he will arrive in New York at 9.00 a.m. He will be able to attend his meeting, or do whatever business he needs, and be back in London the same day. It will be no more trouble than a train journey to the north of England.

Concorde could be the beginning of a new revolution in transport. We must not let a lot of stick-in-the muds prevent it.

An economist, 1981

I objected strongly to Concorde from the outset and now most people agree with me that the project should never have been started.

It is the terrible waste of money that angers me most. In the beginning it was supposed to cost £90 million but before it was finished it was ten times as much. It amounted to £12 a head for every man, woman and child in Britain and France. No-one asked us if we wanted to spend the money. Even if the aircraft had been a success, who would have benefited? A few business men and politicians might have saved a few hours perhaps, while the rest of us might have enjoyed a little more national prestige. In the end we got very little prestige from that venture.

It was ridiculous to claim that Concorde would halve the travelling time from London to New York, because actual flying time was cut down from 7 to $3\frac{1}{2}$ hours. I'm not interested in how long it takes me to fly from Heathrow to Kennedy Airport. I have to get from my home to my hotel on the other side, which means travelling across London and New York. The flying time may be seven hours, but the total travelling time is nearer ten or eleven, even if there are no hold-ups. Three and half hours is one third of the travelling time, not one half. Surely it would have been much more sensible and a lot cheaper to lay on some fast transport from the city centres to the airports and to improve the airports themselves so that people could pass through them more quickly. All passengers would have benefited from that, not just the privileged few that fly Concorde, and I do mean few!

Who needs to save three and a half hours anyway? Whose time can be that valuable? Who finds it essential to go to New York and back in a single day? If anyone's business is as brief as that, surely it could be done by telephone. If a man has to spend two days in New York, then three and a half hours is nothing. He spends much longer than that sleeping off his jet lag.

Also there has been a lot of competition. Our experts said they had stolen a march on the rest of the world and were four years ahead of them. Much of that time was frittered away with industrial disputes and the like. The Russians flew 'Concordski' before Concorde was on the market. The Americans of course were too clever to fall for that supersonic nonsense. Boeing put their resources into jumbo jets that take 500 passengers at 600 miles per hour, which is close enough to the speed of sound. They are much cheaper to fly than Concorde of course. If you have to choose between saving £200 on the fare or three and a half hours on the journey, what would you do?

The main problem has always been sonic boom. You may have heard it from fighter aircraft. There is a crash like a car door slamming, which is quite enough to make anyone jump, and to wake all but the heaviest sleeper. Nor is there just the one bang. The noise is continuous and what is worse, it can be heard for up to thirty miles on either side of the aircraft. Sonic booms cause damage to property as well as people. We are told that buildings which are in good repair do not suffer. Does that mean the others only get what they deserve? You will hardly agree if you are unlucky enough to live in one.

Passenger congestion at London Airport.

A 'Jumbo' (Boeing 747) airliner.

Besides, most of the finest cathedrals are a bit shaky to say the least. It is not surprising that people in many different parts of the world have been against Concorde flying over their countries and landing and taking off from their airports.

Everyone now knows that Concorde, although a wonderful piece of engineering in many ways, has not been a success. It uses far too much expensive fuel for the number of passengers it can carry and for most people the extra speed has not been worth the extra fare. Already it is going out of service on some passenger routes. Certainly the tax payer will never see a return on the huge amount of public money that was spent on this project.

A modern version of the sailing ship; the sail driven oil tanker.

Sea and Air Transport: Conclusion

Over the last two hundred years there has been great progress in sea transport. Instead of little sailing ships of about 300 tons we have motor driven merchant vessels, including oil tankers of over 500,000 tons.

Progress in the air has been even more remarkable. Before 1903 no-one had flown, except in a balloon that had to drift with the wind. Now, thousands of people travel by air every day.

The history of transport is interesting for its failures as well as its successes. It is not just that certain forms of transport, like the sailing ship and the ocean liner, have reached a peak, and then been put out of business. There have also been a number of false starts. The ocean-going iron steam ship was a failure, so was the air ship, and the supersonic aircraft may be one as well.

Questions

1 What invention made it possible to build the great ocean liners? When was their golden age?
2 Describe the development of the aeroplane down to 1960.
3 What choice did aircraft designers have in the 1960s? Why did Britain and France decide to build Concorde?
4 What problems were there with Concorde?
5 Contrast the views of the aeronautical engineer and the economist. With which of these do you agree?

9 The Countryside

The Countryside in the Eighteenth Century

In the medieval village, the land was divided into three. There was the arable, which grew crops, the meadow which grew hay, and the common which was used for summer grazing. The arable itself was also divided into three. These were large fields, about a mile across. One grew wheat for bread, one grew barley, beans and peas for animal feed while the third lay fallow. Each year the use of the fields changed.

The peasants all farmed in the same way, so there were no enclosures, that is hedges or fences, to divide one man's land from his neighbour's. Nor was any individual farm in one piece. Each man would have a few strips of land scattered through the arable fields, a number of meadow 'doles' also well scattered, and he would have the right to graze a number of beasts on the common.

Most medieval farming was what we call 'subsistence' farming. That meant the peasant produced very little for sale. The crops he grew were either food for himself and his family, or for his animals.

Farming was also primitive, but no-one could strike out on his own and make improvements, because, as we have seen, they all worked together.

As time went on, however, some farmers 'engrossed' their holdings. By exchanging strips they managed to get much of their land in large blocks. They then enclosed it by planting hedges round it so that they could farm as they pleased. A progressive man could use new methods, grow food for sale and make himself rich. A lord of the manor would be particularly keen to have large enclosed farms for his tenants, since that meant he could charge higher rents. Most small farmers, though, wanted to keep the old system, and resisted changes. The only way to compel them was to get Parliament to pass an Enclosure Act for the village, and that was very expensive.

Then in the eighteenth century the population

The village of Laxton in Nottinghamshire, where the open-field system survives. The individual strips can be clearly seen in the field in the centre of the picture.

grew and the price of food went up. The rents of large, enclosed farms increased so much that many a landowner felt it worthwhile to go to the trouble and expense of obtaining an Enclosure Act. From the case studies you can see how enclosure affected the landlord, his tenants and the ordinary villagers.

The Lord of the Manor

I say that enclosures are for the good of the nation. Our industries need wool and flax for cloth, woad and madder to make dyes, to say nothing of leather for shoes, saddles and harness. Our towns are growing with the increase in trade, and their people have to be fed. Merchants bring many goods from abroad into the country, and if we are not to squander our gold we must pay for them with exports of grain. Too much land is still held by cottagers and small farmers who eat all that they can grow, but when these little holdings are thrown together to make large, enclosed farms, the produce of the land is doubled. I would not deny that my rents are doubled as well, but I have need of the money. The expense of a great house grows year by year: I have three daughters to marry off and they must have dowries. Also we must entertain as lavishly as the other gentry of this county do.

Of couse I am not the only one to benefit. My tenants have every reason to be content. Here in Broadhampton there were some 3,000 parcels of land before enclosure. A farm was a strip here, a strip there, some well-scattered meadow doles and, perhaps, some common rights. So intermingled were the holdings that everyone had to work together, and that was at the pace of the slowest. A man of spirit could not try new crops, still less would he buy pedigree stock to mix with the scabby beasts which the villagers ran on the common. There were problems, too, with the labourers. When a man has two or three acres, with a cow and perhaps a pig or two, then he will save his energy to take care of what is his own. He will come tired to his labour from having risen early to dig his garden. He will work for his master no more than three days in the week, and that at the busiest season of the year. He may be unruly and disobedient knowing that even if he has no employment, he may at least scratch a bare living from his own holding.

How different things are now! My tenants have compact farms of 200 acres or more, neatly enclosed. The greatest changes of all are on what was the old common. The furze has been uprooted and burnt, the ant hills levelled, the rabbit warrens destroyed and a stagnant swamp drained. It has been ploughed, seeded with new grass and now supports fine herds of beef cattle.

You may ask what has happened to the cottagers and if they have suffered. My answer is that they too have gained from enclosures. I once visited a cottage belonging to a squatter on the common. It was as poor as anything I have ever seen in Ireland.

This is the sort of cottage that a squatter might have lived in, though of much better quality than the one described.

It had been dug out of the slope of a hill. There was just one room. The floor was of earth, the walls were of turf, and the chimney of clay. They could not afford glass, and the window, a mere hole in the wall, had been stuffed with rags to keep out the cold. The bed was a heap of straw on the ground, with a ragged blanket and a bit of sheet. That cottage is no more since the enclosure of the common, and its aged inmates are lodged comfortably in the workhouse. Owning that miserable hovel had only encouraged them to live in misery.

The labourers now have allotments of not more than half an acre so they work full time for the farmers. Their wages are more than they could possibly have made from their wretched little holdings.

As for their common rights to which they clung, I am sure they cost far more than they were worth. Too many cattle were turned onto the common, and there was not enough grass for them. A child would spend all day looking after the family cow and at the end of it the animal would give barely a quart of milk. They used their cows as plough animals, and worked them until they died. By then they were all skin and bone, so there was no meat for the butcher. Anyway, few cottagers grew enough winter feed for their animals, so they had to buy hay in the winter. That must certainly have turned any profit into loss.

The country parson

I have seen many changes in the countryside during my life but few have done so much harm to the poor as the enclosure of the open fields and common. I do not say that the ordinary villagers ever lived well, but at least they had a few modest comforts.

I remember their cottages used to look tidy. Each had its garden with its crops of potatoes, carrots, cabbages and beans. Many had fruit trees. Nearly always there was a sty with a good pig grunting away. A little shed would be full of fuel for the winter. It is true that the cottages were small, some of them no more than one room for the whole family, but they were neatly kept, and their walls whitewashed inside and out every year.

In the fields each family had an acre or two of land on which they grew wheat and barley. The wheat made them bread; the barley they gave to their livestock; the straw they used to thatch their houses and feed their animals through any winter. If by any chance they did not have enough winter feed, all they had to do was buy a little hay.

Their common rights were of even greater value than their garden or their arable, for it was the common that fed their livestock. There was nothing a family prized more than its cow. It gave them milk for their children for nine or ten months of the year, and a little cheese and butter as well, which they might sell for a few pennies. Some villagers kept a sheep or two, and all had geese. From the common they also had turf and furze for firing.

A cottager's garden and his arable might occupy him for no more than two days in the week, so he spent the other four labouring for one of the farmers. If his children were old enough they could watch the beasts on the common, while his wife spent her day spinning. At harvest time she could work in the fields and afterwards there was the gleaning.

How everything has changed! The cottager has lost his strips of land on the open fields. They are now part of the big new farms which we have. The commons are divided into neat fields, and they too belong to the big farms. Each cottager had an allotment of half an acre to compensate him for the loss of his common rights, but what good did that do him? He cannot keep a cow on half an acre! After the enclosure it was indeed a sorry sight to see the poor folk driving their cattle to market, knowing they would never replace them. Some of the allotments were a mile from the village. A man could not go all out there at the end of a day's work. One poor fellow sold his plot to the squire in the end. The squire gave him £10 for it. The man thought it was a fortune at the time and he hid it in a little pot under the floor of the cottage. He spent it all a bit at a time and now he has nothing left.

All that a poor cottager has today are the wages

The parson is describing a way of life that this picture expresses; one of freedom and prosperity for ordinary countryfolk.

that he and his wife can earn. As prices go up year by year, those wages buy less. There are government taxes to be paid on soap and candles, too. Many families live on bread and little else. The farmers only keep beef cattle and the villagers' cows have gone. That means it is hard to find milk for the children. Folk have to walk miles to the woods for a bit of timber so mostly all there is for fuel is wheat stubble and not enough of that. Five families in the village have joined together and take it in turn to light a fire. The wives all do their cooking on the one fire. Most of the winter the houses are cold. Men come in from the fields wet through and have no way of warming themselves or drying their clothes. In the morning they have to put on their wet clothes and go out into the frost or the rain.

There was a time when the villagers would have been ashamed to go to the parish, but now many draw relief almost every winter. They used to get up early and go to bed late so that they could work on their gardens. Now they spend much less time working for themselves. They are not careful with money either. They say they will never be able to buy a cow or a plot of land to grow a few potatoes, so they might as well enjoy their pot of beer while they can. What a sad change in their way of life to be sure!

Questions

1. What fields were there in a medieval village? What land would a farmer have? Why might he wish to 'engross' and 'enclose'?
2. According to the lord of the manor, how did the enclosure benefit the country, his tenants and himself? Why did he say the poor were better off after enclosure?
3. What did the country parson say about the way the poor lived before enclosure? How did he say they suffered after enclosure? How did he differ from the squire? Which do you believe? Why?

This painting, called 'Preparing for dinner', clearly shows a cottage interior.

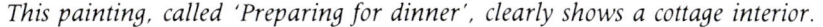

The Countryside in the Nineteenth Century

During the Napoleonic Wars (1793–1815) the price of wheat and most farm goods was so high that farmers found life very easy. After the war, though, prices fell so farmers who wanted to make money had to produce more and more. In order to do that, they had to improve their methods and, thanks to the enclosure movement, they were free to do so.

You will remember that under the old system, one third of the arable had been fallow, but now it was realized that there was no need to waste land in this way. All the land could be cultivated as long as the crops were changed each year. A sequence of crops is called a 'rotation' and there were many different kinds. The best known was the 'Norfolk Four Course' which was especially common in East Anglia. This was wheat, turnips, barley and grasses. Often, however, a farmer would leave the land under grass for two or more years before ploughing it again for wheat. The turnips and the grasses were extra fodder crops which made it possible to keep more animals. The farmer in the first case history explains why this was important for him.

After 1850 the price of farm goods began to go up again and from then until 1870 farmers enjoyed what has been called their 'Golden Age'. Thanks to all the improvements that had been made, they were producing more than they had ever done before, and were selling it at the new high prices: iron was cheap so they could have all the machines they needed: the country had railways which took their goods to market quickly and easily: perhaps most important of all, there was not much competition from abroad. Almost all the food eaten in Britain was grown in Britain.

Landlords benefited as well. Since their tenants were making so much money they charged them even higher rents.

While farmers and landlords were doing well, farm workers were not. The enclosure movement had robbed the poor people of their common rights, so they could no longer keep animals. There were fewer domestic crafts for the country women. Spinning was done in the factories in towns, and you will see what happened to button making in Dorset in the next chapter. But the main problem was that the population had grown, and there were so many labourers that the farmers were able to pay low wages. If a poor family was to live, the women and children had to work, and as you will see in the second case study, much of their labour was hard and disagreeable.

Farmyard. In the days before tractors, horses were most important. Like all farm animals they were much improved by scientific breeding.

Richard Hudson, a farmer at Castle Acre, Norfolk, 1850

I hear there are farmers who complain they cannot make a living because the price of wheat is so low. I agree that it is less than it was during the war against Napoleon. My father has told me that it was then four times as high as today. But there is an answer to that, and it is simply to grow more wheat. A man who sells a hundred quarters of wheat at forty shillings a quarter, has as much money as another who sells fifty quarters at eighty shillings a quarter. I grow twice as much wheat as my father did, from the same amount of land. Also I keep far more sheep and cattle than he did.

One reason I prosper is that I have such a large farm—1,500 acres altogether. No small farmer could afford to do all the things that I do.

I follow a proper plan of cropping. I have divided my farm into five, and the use of each piece changes every year. First comes wheat, next turnips, and the third year barley. Along with the barley I sow clover and grasses which remain when the barley is harvested. In the fourth year the clover and grasses give me a handsome crop of hay and in the fifth year I use the land for summer grazing. One golden rule is never to take straw crops from the same land two years following. Another is not to allow land to remain long either in tillage or in pasture.

I sell my wheat, of course, but the turnips, barley, hay and grass are all fodder for my livestock. They increase year by year. My father kept 400 sheep and 30 bullocks. I now have 2,500 sheep and 150 bullocks. I am grateful for this because while the price of grain has been falling, the price of meat has held up very well.

As you can imagine, I have a great deal of manure from these animals. All my land is manured every year, while the clover has no less than eight cart loads to the acre. Here is the grand secret of my success. The more crops I grow, the more animals I keep: the more animals I keep, the more manure I have: the more manure I have the heavier are my crops.

I would not have you believe that I think ill of my father. Though he produced barely one half of what I do, he was an excellent farmer who taught me my business well, but I have advantages which he did not.

There are artificial fertilizers for one thing. I set great store by superphosphates. I have found that a light sprinkling of this wonderful powder will increase my wheat crops by almost a quarter. Some folk now say that farmers will one day manage with artificial fertilizers alone. For my part I cannot believe they will ever replace dung, but I have proved many times over that they help it a good deal.

The railway is a great boon to me. Formerly our animals had to walk to London, and I worked out that each sheep lost seven pounds in weight, and each bullock twenty-eight pounds. The total loss to me every year was upwards of £600. Now the railway takes the stock to London in a single day and all that expense is saved.

I also have my steam engine of course. It turns a driving shaft to which I can attach all manner of machines, such as my chaff cutter, my turnip slicer, and most important of all, my thrashing machine. In my father's day it took six labourers the entire winter to thrash out the wheat crop using flails. My machine does all that work in three days, and at a fraction of the cost.

I am afraid that labourers do not always see the value of machinery. Back in 1830 we had riots in some parts of England and many thrashing machines were smashed. Here in Norfolk Lord Leicester raised a troop of mounted men which I gladly joined. We soon dealt with the rioters, some of whom were tried and hanged. They were very misguided men. Though I have a thrasher, in fact I give work to far more people than my father did. There are many tasks on the farm that can never be mechanized. Who could ever invent a device that would harvest wheat? To bring in my corn, I employ no less than thirty-two mowers, and each needs two women to help him, one to gather the wheat, and the other to bind the sheaves. No, I am sure that the more farming progresses, the more workers it will employ.

Cross section of a thrashing machine. Hudson's thrashing machine would have been like this.

The Countryside

A farm labourer's daughter of Castle Acre, Norfolk, 1850

My name is Jane Sculfer and I am fourteen. My father is a labourer on Mr. Hudson's farm. We live in a cottage in Castle Acre. It is one of a row and is very small with just two rooms, one upstairs and one down. There are six children in our family, and we all have to sleep in the same bedroom with our parents. Father and mother are in one bed, with the baby, my two brothers have another bed, and I share a third with my two sisters.

I went to school until I was twelve, so I can read and write a little. Mother can as well, but my father not at all.

I can't say that we often go hungry, but our food is nearly always the same. For breakfast I have some flour, with a little butter, and water from the tea kettle poured over it. I take my dinner with me to my work. It is just a hunk of bread but sometimes I have a bit of cheese as well. When we come home in the evening we all have potatoes, and if we are lucky, a bit of bacon. If there are cabbages in the garden mother will boil one in the pot with the potatoes and bacon. Once, she did not notice there was a toad in the cabbage. It was cooked along with our supper and we were all very ill.

Father's wages are only eight shillings a week, and he has to pay a shilling of that as rent for the cottage. If the family is to live, then the children must work. I work for Mr. Fuller who is a gangmaster. He has a gang of thirty, all women and children. He arranges with a farmer like Mr. Hudson to do a certain job for him for a sum of money and then sets us to work. In the winter we pick up stones from the fields. Sometimes they are frozen to the ground and it is hard to loosen them with bare fingers. We put them in buckets and then empty the buckets into a cart. I have often hurt my back carrying the buckets. In spring we hoe the wheat, and that's not too bad, for there is no bending or stooping. Next comes the harvest. The women and girls follow the mowers and tie the wheat into sheaves. It is hard going, I can tell you, but I enjoy

'The Harvest Waggon' by Stubbs. Jane could be one of the girls.

harvest time. Everyone is happy. The farmer sends beer out to the fields, and in the evening we sit down at long tables in the barn and have a good supper. In the autumn we have the job I hate most of all, and that is lifting turnips. The little ones are bad enough, but the big ones can weigh seven pounds. It is as much as I can do to wrench them out of the ground, and my hands are covered in blisters long before the day is out. I often leave the house crying during the turnip lifting.

Fuller pays each of us sixpence a day wages, but only if we work the whole day. Sometimes we have to stop in the morning because the weather turns bad. A good deal of work may have been done, and though the farmer pays Fuller for it, we get nothing.

One bad thing about working with a gang is that I often have to go far from home. Father has to walk a mile to Mr. Hudson's farm and he grumbles enough about that. But Fuller contracts for farmers up to six miles away. Often I have to leave home at six in the morning and in the summer may not come back before nine in the evening.

When he heard I was going to work in Fuller's gang, the Rector was very worried. He saw my parents about it and read me a stern lecture. He warned me that there were a lot of bad boys in the gang and said I must be sure to behave myself. I don't know what mischief he thinks I could get up to. Fuller keeps us spaced out across the fields lest we should gossip rather than work. At the end of the day it is as much as I can do to make my way home. Often I drop straight into bed, too tired to have supper.

Questions

1. Why did a farmer of 1850 wish to produce much more food than one who lived in 1800?
2. What advantages did the farmer of 1850 enjoy? What system of cropping did he follow? Why did the weight of his crops and the numbers of his animals grow together?
3. What did farm labourers feel about machinery?
4. Describe Jane Sculfer's home and home life. What work did she do through the seasons? How would she have felt if her employer had bought machines to do much of the work?

A group of farm labourers taken not long after the period that Jane describes.

The Countryside in the Twentieth Century

The prairies of North America are some of the best land in the world, but for a long time no-one could do much with them. Anyone who had tried to farm them would have been without labour, and the means of transporting his goods. Then the reaper binder was invented which not only cut wheat but tied it into sheaves. That went a long way towards solving the labour problem. Also railways and steamships were built, and they solved the transport problem. Farming on the prairies was at last possible, and it grew rapidly. From the 1870s onwards Canada and the United States had large amounts of cheap food which they exported to Britain.

In Britain most people were only too pleased to have cheap food from North America, but for farmers it was a disaster. Some of them went over to milk production, but others let their land go to waste. Most of Britain's food came from abroad.

During the First World War, however, the German U-boats sank many ships in the North Atlantic so it was important that Britain should grow as much of her own food as possible. Farming revived and farmers prospered once more. Since the Second World War particularly, the government has helped them, and on the whole they have continued to do well. Farmers have helped themselves, too, by using new methods and buying elaborate, expensive machines like combine harvesters. Farming is now a highly technical, scientific business, and more food is produced per acre than ever before.

But the countryside still has its problems. Because farmers are using so many machines, they do not need workers, so men have had to move into towns. As a result many villages are dying. Often, only the old folk remain, and they find life more and more difficult as you will see in the case studies. Another problem has been caused by the motor car. If there is a town nearby then people who have jobs there may quite easily live in the village and drive to and from their work. Then the village does not die, but it does change its character. Instead of being a community of farmers and farm workers, who all know each other, it becomes a dormitory for a city. The newcomers are quite different from the country families. They may find they have difficulties in living alongside them, even though they do their best to fit in and help.

A wheatfield in Wiltshire; one of the new, large fields suitable for 'prairie farming'.

Mrs. Forrester—an Oxfordshire farm worker's widow

I have seen many changes in the village since I was a little girl, and few of them for the better.

The countryside is being ruined. One of the first things that happened was that great row of pylons striding across the fields. They were built back in the 1930s. Then came the war and since then there has been quite a new spirit in farming. It seems that farmers cannot bear to have a bit of wet ground, a few bushes or even a hedgerow. You can see that hole there, with the broken car and all the tin cans. It used to be a pond, with frogs and newts and all kinds of insects. So many trees have died too. It is a shame. The elms were killed by Dutch Elm disease, but the oaks are going as well. They tell me it's because the farmers have drained the land so well that the trees cannot find enough moisture.

Two other features of the countryside; pylons and people on horses.

The fields used to be quite small, with thick hedgerows, full of birds' nests, and banks covered with wild flowers. Many of these hedges have been grubbed up. That gives the farmers more land, you see, and it is easier for them to use their machines in the big empty fields.

But even the fields have changed. They used to be in pasture all the time, and so many different grasses grew in them. I had a scrap book full of specimens I had dried and preserved. There were ryegrass, foxtails, cocksfoot, meadow brome, quaking grass, oh, and lots more. There were flowers too, like cowslips, as well as many beautiful butterflies. Now the meadows have been ploughed and smothered with chemicals. Some of the land grows crops and some just dull, ordinary grass. There are no butterflies, of course. The farmers' sprays have killed them all.

In the old days there was a common near the village where children picked blackberries or played by the stream. The bracken was always a lovely colour in the autumn. It is all ploughed up now, and divided with those horrible electric fences. There is a footpath across it, but we had to fight to keep it open.

I don't like the changes in the village either. New families keep moving in. The more ordinary ones live on a fancy little housing estate, but there are rich newcomers as well. Some buy cottages and keep them just for the weekends while others buy the nice old houses and make them look smart. Between them they drive up the prices of property so that they are too high for the local people. My grandson and his wife and baby have had to go and live in a council house on the edge of the village. What is more, so many of the new people do not really belong. They live here it's true, but they work in town, shop in town and they go to town for their entertainment. Our village is not much more than a place where they sleep.

Another disaster is the big four-lane highway, which they are building near my house. The noise of the machinery is dreadful, and so will the noise of the traffic be I'm sure. They take the common for farmland, then they take the farmland for roads. It just doesn't make sense to me.

It's nearly impossible to find work here. My grandson is lucky to have a job as a cowman, but the farmers have so many machines that they hardly need men. Most of the young people have to move. All that are left are the elderly, like me, and these new people who don't really belong.

For those of us that are old, life becomes more and more of a problem. What happens if I am ill?

A new housing estate in a village.

My doctor belongs to a group practice in a larger village. I can't go and see him, and he doesn't want to come all out here every time I have a bit of rheumatism. If he does, and gives me a prescription, how do I get it made up? The nearest chemist is ten miles away, and there is no bus even if I was fit enough to use it. They closed our sub-post office, so that collecting the old age pension is another problem. Shopping is difficult too. Mrs. Brown who keeps our only store says she is losing money so she cuts down on her goods. The trouble is that the more she cuts down the less she sells, so it gets worse all the time. Anyway all her things are so expensive!

I feel sorry for the children—the few that are left. Our village school was closed some years ago, so

The old village shop. What do you like or dislike about a shop like this?

the children have to go elsewhere by bus. The older ones tell me they spend an hour on the bus morning and evening as it has to travel to all the villages for miles around. Oh dear, it's all very different from when I was a girl.

Mr. Thompson, a new resident in the village

I am an accountant, and I work in a large town twenty miles away. I moved here with my family about five years ago, and I must say we have never regretted it. We found this rather derelict old house but its walls were sound and it had a lovely stone roof. Inside we more or less gutted it and modernized it completely. It cost me thousands of pounds, but now the place must be worth several times the price I paid for it. You can see it has a splendid garden for the children to play in when they are home from boarding school.

We find plenty to do here. There are lots of nice walks and I enjoy a bit of fishing. The children are learning to ride and my wife likes gardening. I do admit, though, that this is not the place to be without a car. Still, my Jaguar takes me to my office in about half an hour, and it will be quite a bit quicker when the new road is finished. My wife has a little car, too, and she does need it, especially for shopping. The village shop is really terrible – just Oxo cubes and tins of baked beans. Fortunately there is a splendid hypermarket on the outskirts of town and it's no trouble for Jane to drive there once a week and stock up. The deep freeze is a great help, of course.

Sometimes we are a little bored with the pleasures of the countryside, but we just slip into town to a play or a concert. There is usually something going on.

Mind you, I think if you live in a place you should be part of it. Jane and I have done our best, even though the local people weren't too welcoming at first. Jane has a couple of old ladies she helps. She collects their shopping lists from them every Tuesday, and buys all they need at the hypermarket. That saves them a few pounds in the year I can tell you, but they still grumble about the price of things. Then she draws their old age pensions for them, and if the doctor leaves either of the old dears a prescription she is usually on her way to collect it from the nearest chemist within the hour.

I do my bit, too. A lot of trees have died lately, so on Saturday afternoons a group of us goes out and plants saplings in the hedgerows. We shall never see them as grown trees, but our grandchildren will.

An old village house 'converted' for the benefit of a well-off city commuter.

I was also Chairman of the action group that managed to keep open the footpath across the old common. I am a member of the Parish Council as well. A parish council does not have a lot of power, but we keep nagging the County Council about the things that concern us. What bothers me most about this village and many others is that there are too many retired people and not enough young couples. Housing is part of the problem. There should be more new houses suitable for young people to buy. The trouble is that houses are no use without jobs. Many people find they cannot afford to drive twenty

An aerial view of a hypermarket. Note the large car parking area.

Most city-dwellers' idea of a typical English village.

What a typical village is really like.

miles to their work every day. Farmers don't need workers any more and I really don't know what sort of industry would thrive in a place like this.

There are other problems too. The towns need cheap food which means scientific farming: they need electricity which comes in on those huge pylons: they need cheap transport which means motorways. One mile of motorway takes thirty acres of land you know. We can't have all these things in the countryside and keep it 'olde worlde' and lovely. Yet when the townsfolk go out for a drive that is how they expect to find it!

Still, we must look on the bright side. How many miles of canal have been renovated? How many country houses are open to the public? How many acres of National Park are there? I don't know. But I do know that anyone who is determined to enjoy the English countryside can still do so.

single day.

However, the countryside has always had its problems. When the landowners made enclosures the poor folk lost their right to graze animals on the common and what little land they had as well. During the middle years of the nineteenth century, when the farmers enjoyed a 'golden age', the farm workers remained poor. So many of them competed for jobs that wages were low. After that, it was the turn of the farmers to suffer because of imports of food from abroad. During and since the two World Wars farmers have done well, but there are new difficulties. Since farmers have so many machines, ordinary people have to move into the towns to find work. At the same time, towns people who can afford cars are moving into the country. These changes are making new problems for the families who have always been there.

The Countryside: Conclusion

In the last two hundred years there has been a great deal of progress in farming. For example, at harvest time in the eighteenth century a whole team of reapers cut the corn in a field and women followed to tie the corn into sheaves. After the harvest six or so men spent the winter threshing. Today, one man with a combine harvester can do all that work in a

Questions

1. Why did the development of farming on the prairies harm farming in Britain?
2. When and why did British farming revive?
3. What changes in the countryside did Mrs Forrester regret? What problems did she say country people faced?
4. Why did the Thompsons move to the village? How did they try to help the village? What did Mr Thompson see as the main problems of the countryside?
5. Why would Mrs Forrester have been unwilling to make friends with Mr and Mrs Thompson?

10 Industry

Industry in the Eighteenth Century

During the eighteenth century every part of Britain had its own industry. In Lancashire they made cotton cloth, and in the East of England, East Anglia and Yorkshire they made woollen cloth. These were the most important industries, but there were many others. In parts of Devon they made lace, in Derbyshire stockings, in Worcestershire gloves and in East Dorset, buttons. Most industries were run by merchants, who bought the raw materials and sold the finished goods. Such a merchant might own a few workshops or small mills for some parts of the work, though most of it was done by workers in their own homes. They collected materials from the merchant's agent, made them up at home and then returned the finished articles. We call this the 'domestic system'. Most of the workers were farm labourers' wives and it suited them very well. Labourers were badly paid, so the families were glad of the wives' earnings. Also, the women could look after their houses as well as doing their jobs.

Not all eighteenth century industries used the domestic system, and iron was one of them. At first, though, iron works were quite small. Usually, there was no more than a small blast furnace and a forge. A handful of men and boys could run it quite easily. Iron was smelted in the Forest of Dean and the Weald of Kent and Sussex. In these areas there were iron ore, plenty of oak trees to make charcoal for fuel and water power to drive the blast furnace bellows and trip hammers.

Then, in 1708, Abraham Darby of Coalbrookdale in Shropshire, found out how to smelt iron with coke instead of charcoal. This was important because later in the century the country wanted more iron than could have been made with charcoal. There were just not enough trees. Coke smelting was only the first of many discoveries by the Darby family and the Coalbrookdale works grew into a large business. Other iron works soon followed. You will see from the case study how important iron was for

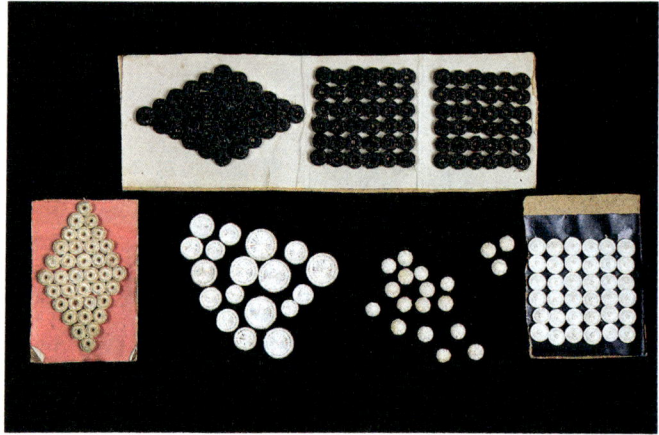

A selection of Dorset buttons from the Dorchester museum.

many things, especially transport and the steam engine. It was the first of our modern industries.

Peter Case, a Dorset button manufacturer

Buttony began in Dorset when my ancestor Abraham Case came to live in Blandford back in 1622. There were a lot of sheep in Dorset, then, as there are now. Abraham wondered if anything could be done with the sheeps' horns. What he did was to slice them into fine rings, and cover them with cloth to make buttons. For fancy buttons all you had to do was embroider the cloth. My ancestor was soon in business. When Charles I went to his execution in 1649 he had Case buttons on his waistcoat. That was a splendid advertisement for the firm.

Early this century we had a problem because more and more people wanted our buttons. Slicing up sheep horns takes a long time and there is a limit to their number, even in this county. My father found the answer was to have wire rings. We use them all the time now. The wire comes in broad wheeled waggons, all the way from Birmingham.

I have a workshop at Shaftesbury and another at Bere Regis. Nearly all the work is done by children. First of all a winder twists a piece of hot wire round a rod, to make something like a spring. He then snips it down its full length, so that it falls apart into

A broad-wheeled waggon, the kind used for bringing wire from Birmingham to Dorset.

This pub near Blandford, Dorset was once a depot where finished buttons would be delivered on 'Button Day'.

a score of broken rings. After that a dipper dips the ends into molten solder to join them together. Last of all, a stringer threads the rings onto bits of string, a gross at a time. I am afraid winders and dippers often burn themselves. They should be more careful. The important work is casting and filling. 'Casting' means covering the rings with linen cloth, and 'filling' is embroidering patterns on the buttons. Each pattern has its own name. There are Mites and Spangles, which are very small buttons, and there are High Tops for hunting waistcoats. Others are Yannells, Bird's Eyes, Honeycombs, Dorset Knobs and Blandford Cartwheels. Altogether there are about a hundred different fillings, so there is plenty of choice.

Well, we have been able to speed up the ring manufacture, but I'm quite certain we shall never speed up the casting and filling. There is no point in building expensive workshops for these jobs, so we employ women to do them in their own homes. I have depots all over the east of the county. Mostly, they are rooms in public houses. One of my agents will visit a depot once a week. 'Button Day' people call it. The agent gives rings, linen and thread to the women, and they bring in the finished buttons. My agent pays them for their work, of course, and there are some lively arguments about that from time to time.

The buttons all come back to my workshops where they are sorted and sewn on to cards. Seconds go on yellow cards, standard buttons on blue cards and the superior ones on pink. We export the standard and superior buttons and sell off the seconds cheaply to local people.

Buttony has brought prosperity to east Dorset. I employ a thousand women and children, mainly the families of farm labourers. A labourer earns about twelve shillings a week. His wife, if she works hard, may make a gross of buttons a day and if these are of the superior sort I will pay her four shillings for them. Alas, very few women are industrious enough to do that regularly. Some are slovenly and make only seconds, worth a mere five pence a gross. One problem with the women is that they have other things to do. They look after their homes and families, and the farmers sometimes persuade them to work in the fields. Everyone enjoys harvesting, so they are very willing to help with that. There are very few buttons made in Dorset during the harvest time, I can assure you. Most of the year, though, the average button maker will earn as much working for me, as her husband will, labouring on a farm. I am pleased to say that schoolchildren and paupers in workhouses also do buttony and earn money for their establishments.

We must be grateful to the cotton manufacturers of Lancashire for all this. While they are making cloth by the mile, people will need buttons by the thousand. The cloth goes all over the world and my buttons with it. I do a lot of business in Liverpool and have made sure my name will never be forgotten there. I have built a street of handsome houses and called it 'Case's Street'.

Industry

Abraham Darby, ironmaster of Coalbrookdale

My grandfather, also called Abraham Darby like me, was the first of our family to make iron at Coalbrookdale. He moved here in 1709, and leased the old Blast Furnace, or No. 1 Furnace as we call it. It was the only one in the valley then, and it was not as big as it is now.

In those days everyone used brass cooking pots, imported from Holland. Brass is expensive, of course, so grandfather asked himself if the pots could be made in iron, which was a great deal cheaper and just as good. The problem was that the fuel they used for smelting iron was charcoal, which gave barely enough heat. The iron came oozing out of the furnace like toffee. You could cast a fire back with it, but for a shape like a pot it needed to flow much more freely. Grandfather decided he would try smelting iron with coke, which gives a much higher temperature. In the end he succeeded and soon his iron pots were on sale in fairs and markets all over the country.

These days, ironmasters everywhere have reason to bless my grandfather. In Britain we now make so much more iron than we did early in the century, that we could not possibly grow enough timber to smelt it all. There seems to be no limit to the coal we can mine, so there will be no limit to the iron we can make.

Coalbrookdale is a good place for a furnace as it lies between the ore and the coal in the hills above us and the River Severn down below. Our materials come down hill to the furnace, and then our castings go on down hill to the river. At no point do we have to haul heavy loads up steep slopes. There have been problems, though. By the middle of the century, in my father's day, the business had grown so much that it was producing a hundred tons of iron a week. Each ton of iron needs six or seven times its own weight of ore and coke, so the works used something like a hundred tons of materials every day. All that had to be brought here by pack horses, and the most any of those beasts could carry was $2\frac{1}{2}$ cwt. The answer was to build railways, as they have for the coalmines of the north of England.

Coalbrookdale, one of the places where the Industrial Revolution began.

At first, our rails were of oak, and were always breaking or splitting. Then, late in the 1760s, trade became slack and we could not sell our iron. We did not wish to blow out our furnaces and dismiss our men, but what could we do with our iron? Someone suggested we should cast it into iron plates and lay them on the wooden rails. When trade revived we could take up the plates and use the iron for castings. In fact, the iron plates did the job so well that we have never taken them up. We have about twenty miles of railway in the works, and we now make plates for sale.

Another problem was water. If the pond ran dry, the water-wheel would stop and we would have to blow out the furnace. There is an old man here who remembers a run of dry years in the 1730s. Customers were demanding iron, but none could be made. In those days, the only remedy was patience. Since 1740 we have had a steam engine. After the water has turned the wheel, the engine pumps it back to the pond. It does its work over and over again until the drought ends.

Today we have other steam engines, to drive the machinery in our forges. They are useful, but I cannot say that they will ever replace the water wheel entirely. The waterwheel is so simple that it does not break down, and is very cheap to run.

We still make pots, as my grandfather did, and we sell them all over the world. Some only hold a pint or two, but others, that we send to Africa, are so huge you could boil a man in one. We call them 'missionary pots'. Today most of our business is making steam engines. They grow ever bigger. The largest cylinders my father cast were 40" across. My largest are over six feet. A man may stand in them with both arms outstretched. We sell these engines to coal mines, to pump them dry.

Our latest venture is to build an iron bridge over the Severn. Here the river runs through a gorge, so boats cross it with difficulty, and there are timber and limestone on the other side that we need. We have enlarged our Old Blast Furnace and every day we cast twenty tons of iron into ribs, some of them eighty feet long. No-one has built an iron bridge before, but I am determined to try.

Cooking pots, manufactured by the first Abraham Darby.

Questions

1 How was the Dorset button industry organized? What problems did Peter Case have with his business?
2 How did button making help the poor of East Dorset? Why did farmers dislike it?
3 When and why did Abraham Darby find how to smelt iron with coke? Why was his discovery important later on?
4 What were the other main achievements of the Coalbrookdale Iron Company in the eighteenth century?

Ironbridge, over the River Severn.

Industry in the Nineteenth Century

During the nineteenth century the 'domestic system' came to an end in most industries. Instead, goods were made in factories as they are today. The cotton industry was one of the first to make the change, and we will see what happened here.

For the manufacturer, the domestic system had several disadvantages. His workers were scattered over a wide area, perhaps even through several counties. Giving them their raw materials and collecting the finished goods was so complicated that he had to employ 'putters out'. Also, domestic workers were unreliable. They did not finish their work on time, sometimes it was badly done, and sometimes the materials were stolen. Finally, it was not possible to speed up production with machines because only simple equipment would fit into a cottage home. Fortunately for the manufacturers a number of things happened which made it possible for them to have factories.

In the first place, thanks to people like the Darbys of Coalbrookdale, there was plenty of iron. This was used to make fireproof buildings and machines. Secondly, there were new sources of power. Inventors like John Smeaton had designed improved water wheels. Also, James Watt had developed an efficient steam engine. Steam power was not common until after 1850, but a manufacturer would use it if it was not possible to build his factory near a fast-flowing stream. Thirdly, there were several important inventions. The first were the spinning machines. In 1769 Richard Arkwright patented his 'water frame', so called because it needed a water wheel to drive it. Ten years later Samuel Crompton invented his 'mule' which spun a finer thread than the water frame. In the end there were mules that could spin a thousand threads at a time.

Weaving is more complicated than spinning, so it took longer to develop a power loom. That was finally done in the early nineteenth century. All the work of making cotton cloth could now be done in a factory.

The new factories meant jobs for many people, so large towns grew up around them. But what happened to the domestic workers? Farm labourers' wives could no longer spin in their own homes so their families were much poorer. The handloom weavers tried to compete with power looms, earning less and less money for more and more hours of work. In the end they had to give up.

What happened in cotton happened also in most other industries. For example, button making in Dorset came to an end soon after 1850. A Birmingham man called Ashton had invented a button-making machine.

Arkwright's cotton mill, still operating after two hundred years.

A Lancashire cotton manufacturer in the 1830s

My mill was finished in 1834. It is one of the most modern in Lancashire. We take in the raw materials, cotton, bleaching powder, dyestuffs and so on, and we send out finished cloth all ready to be sold.

You can see how large the mill is, some 300 feet long and seven storeys high. Not so long ago it would have been quite unsafe to have a building that size, because of the danger of fire. My father has told me about the spectacular and costly mill fires in his day. Floors were all made of wood, you see, as were the machines. Then they had lamps that dripped oil, so it was easy to start a blaze. In my mill there are iron girders, instead of beams, and the floors are of brick. Machines are made of iron nowadays, of course. We have gas jets for lighting.

The right temperature is important for spinning and so there are iron pipes carrying steam everywhere. They warm not only the cotton but the workers as well, so they are comfortable all the year round. My only problem is to make them open the windows. Their houses are so cold that they stuff every crack they can find with rags and the whole family huddles together in one room. I swear they

Inside a cotton mill. The spinner is helped by two children; a 'piecer' who mends any broken threads, and a 'scavenger' who sweeps up the dust.

would sooner suffocate than suffer the slightest draught.

There are still some mills that use water wheels. I would as well, if it were possible, because wheels are now made that will do the work of a hundred horses. Alas, it is hard to find a site for a wheel like that so I have a pair of steam engines, each of 80 horse power. One great advantage with them is that you can build your mill where you like. Mine is in Bolton where I can find all the workers I need. The Pennine valleys may be good for waterwheels, but no-one wants to live there.

I have seen many changes in the textile industry during my life, but none, I think, is as important as the use of machines for weaving. Spinning has been done by machines for many years now, of course. My father built a spinning mill before the war. I went into the business as a young man, and well remember the problems. We made yarn by the mile, and it had to be delivered to our handloom weavers who were scattered over three counties. There were hundreds of them, some working for as many as four employers. We could not possibly deal with them all, so we employed agents or 'putters out' as the people called them. They took the yarn and contracted to return it woven into cloth. They had no salaries so they made their own bargains with the weavers. Hard bargains they were, too, I believe. Folk round here used to say of a disaster 'It'ud melt the heart of a whetstone, or what's harder, a putter-out'.

Neither weavers nor putters out were reliable. No weaver would do anything on a Monday, he might attempt a little on Tuesday and then try to make up for lost time with a frantic burst of overwork at the end of the week. Usually, he failed. On Saturday he would go to the warehouse to deliver his finished cloth and collect more yarn, so no weaving was done on that day. It was rare for us to deliver an order on time, and we often had to deal with angry customers.

Many of the weavers were dishonest, I'm afraid. They would sell the yarn and then complain that the putter-out had weighed their allowance wrongly.

Weaving is complicated so it wasn't easy to invent a power loom. Horrocks was making them by the 1820s, but I think he used the ideas of several other men. Now power looms are quite common, and we can even weave patterns with the help of Jacquard cards. I have a thousand power looms, tended by 120 adults and about 500 children. I would need ten thousand workers using handlooms to weave the same amount of cloth, and no one firm could ever employ so many.

You must understand that a man like me, who introduces new machines, puts his life at risk. Early this century several mills including our own, were attacked by armed gangs calling themselves Luddites. The yeomanry and the hangman put paid to them but there are still some dangerous men at large. I have been threatened many times, and dare not go out alone at night through fear of having vitriol (concentrated sulphuric acid) thrown in my face. It is the handloom weavers that cause all the trouble. My power looms are putting them out of work. You may ask why I do not employ them in my factory. I did try with a few, but they were so used to working just as and when they pleased, that they could not accept the regular factory hours. Nor could I use their skills, as power looms are quite different from handlooms. I would far rather engage a country lad, straight from the plough, and teach him the trade my way.

A handloom weaver of 1840

I became a weaver back in 1810. That was thirty years ago, when I was a young man. Weaving was a good trade in those days, but gradually the factories have killed it.

When I first started, I could earn 18 shillings a week without working myself too hard. On Sunday I went to church. Monday was a day of rest, and Saturday was an easy day, for that was when I went to the warehouse. I had a garden, I kept a pig and I had plenty of time to look after them. I was able to take my wife to the fair, when it came, or to a dance, for we had the leisure and money for both. The food we ate was plain enough, but wholesome. We had milk, bacon, cheese, eggs and plenty of bread. We ate meat at least once a week. I had three good suits, a number of hats, and a watch in my pocket. Jane, my wife, had several dresses. We made a handsome pair when we went to church on Sundays. Jane always kept our house clean and neat and we had some good furniture, even a mahogany table and dresser.

How times have changed now! If I work for sixteen hours a day, for seven days a week I can hardly earn seven shillings. More often than not, I have no work, and I earn nothing. There is no money for enjoyment now, nor is there time. Even though I may be idle, Jane has to work in a factory, and she is there ten or twelve hours a day. For that, she earns five shillings a week. Our food is of the worst. We have oatmeal and water for breakfast, flour and a little skimmed milk for dinner and oatmeal and water again for supper. There are many days when we can only afford one meal. I am losing my strength and I'm often ill. I haven't money for a doctor so I just work myself well again. The only clothes we have are the ones we stand up in and all of them have been given to us. I forget when we last bought any. We had to sell all our fine furniture when our children were growing up. Our table is just a plain deal board and we sit on boxes. We never go to church now. We are so shabby we would be ashamed to be seen there.

There are many reasons for our misery. I can do skilled work, weaving fine, patterned fabrics on a

This is the membership card of the Amalgamated Society of Operative Cotton Spinners, one of the early Trade Unions.

Jacquard loom. That is difficult, but plain weaving is easily mastered. When it was possible to make good money at it, all sorts of people were eager to learn and learn it they did. There were then too many weavers so the masters were able to force the wages down. I blame the Irish most of all. They came crowding into Lancashire, and as they had woven linen at home, they soon took to weaving cotton over here. What is misery to us, is comfort to them after their mud huts in the bogs of Ireland. They are content with the lowest of wages and that makes things difficult for other weavers.

Then there are the putters-out. If the price of a piece of work is six shillings in their town, they will look somewhere else where labour is plentiful and cheap and have it done for five shillings. We must take the five shillings, or have nothing to do. Even when a piece of cloth is finished it does not follow you will get your brass for it. A putter-out will make abatements if he can. Once, when I had been weaving to a regular pattern, a putter-out refused to pay me. He said I had not done as he asked. He had not told me to change the pattern, but he blamed me for the mistake. In the end I persuaded him to pay me half, but that was all he would give me.

The main problem is the power looms. Men like me are working against fire and water so we are bound to lose. The government should put a tax on the cloth from power looms so that we can compete more fairly.

It will not surprise you to know I am a Chartist. Nor am I one of the milk and water 'moral force' Chartists. I am a 'physical force' man. Only revolution will change the government, and only fear of death will change the factory masters. I long for the day when Captain Swing shall take command in the manufacturing districts.

Questions

1 What made it possible for manufacturers to end the domestic system?
2 What was done to make a cotton mill safe and efficient?
3 What complaints did the cotton manufacturer have about the domestic system. What advantages did he claim for power looms? What risks did he run by using them?
4 How had the handloom weaver's life changed? What reasons did he give for his misfortunes? What political party did he join? What were its aims?

On 10 April 1848, thousands of Chartists met on Kennington Common and marched to Parliament to present their Charter. This photograph of the meeting is one of the earliest crowd photographs ever taken.

Industry in the Twentieth Century

In the eighteenth and early nineteenth centuries most factories used water power, which meant they had to be built by the sides of rivers and streams. In the second half of the nineteenth century, they used steam power, so they were built on the coalfields. These are in the Lowlands of Scotland, the north of England, the Midlands and South Wales. It was here that important industries grew up. There was coalmining itself, the manufacture of iron and steel, textiles, especially cottons and woollens, heavy engineering and ship building. Meanwhile regions like the south of England were still agricultural.

In the twentieth century, there was yet another new source of power, electricity. This can be carried almost anywhere quite easily, so new factories were built, many of them in the south of England. The goods these factories produced were new as well. There were man-made fibres, like rayon, and later, nylon; there were complicated engineering goods like machine tools:there were electrical goods such as washing machines; there were motor cars.

As manufacturers wanted to make as many goods as possible they used 'mass production'. There was nothing very new about this. Many years ago people had discovered what the eighteenth century writer Adam Smith called the 'division of labour'. If you have something which is at all complicated to make, the best thing to do is to divide the process into a large number of simple jobs. One man does each of these, and he can soon learn to work quickly. In the twentieth century, this was carried to the limit by the use of the 'production line' in the motor industry. The assembly of a motor car was broken down into several hundred different and very simple operations. The vehicle was placed on a moving belt which went past the workers just fast enough to give each one time to do his job. An American, Henry Ford, was the first to use the assembly line for cars, but English manufacturers like Henry Austin and Herbert Morris soon copied him.

Mass production may be efficient, but it is very unpleasant for the workers. They have no pleasure or satisfaction in their work which is dull and unskilled. Partly because of this, there has been a great deal of trouble in British factories since the Second World War.

This railway poster from the 1920s, was one of a series showing different British industries.

A car assembly line in the 1960s.

A shop steward in the motor industry, 1960s

When I first came here, things were pretty bad. The supervisors used to treat the lads like dirt. I don't think a supervisor should put himself above anyone else, and if one of them tried to push me around he soon found I could give him plenty of trouble. The other men saw this and they asked me to be their shop steward. I have been one ever since.

You really need tough stewards in this place. There is the job itself for a start. Until you have tried it you can have no idea what it's like to do the same thing over and over again, day after day, week after week. Nor is it light, easy work. Installing suspension units is no fun at all. They weigh twenty-five pounds each, and you are bending down all day. Another bad job is fitting headlamps. You sit on a little trolley, with your head under the wheel arches, and the line pushes you along.

Then there is a bad tradition in this company. It began in America before the First World War. In those days the firm belonged to one family, and their word was law. They would have nothing to do with trade unions. When someone suggested to the workers that they should form a union, the bosses had him beaten up by their thugs. They kept throwing him into the air and dropping him on the concrete. Nothing like that has happened in England but we have had to fight the same mentality. The company did not recognize trade unions until after the Second World War. The people at Union headquarters are no help to us anyway. When we ring to speak to someone, he can't tell us anything. The union officials are all a lot of windbags. The Labour Pary is an even bigger joke. What have they ever done for the workers? We are on our own. We have to look after ourselves.

I can tell you just a few things we have had to fight against. Speeding up is one of them. Suppose the line was fixed to move at thirty cars an hour. That gave each man two minutes to do his own particular job. After a while, though, he would find something wrong. He couldn't work up the line and earn himself a few minutes rest for a ciggie. The reason was that the line had been speeded up to thirty-five cars an hour. The lads clubbed together and bought me a stop-watch and we ended that game. I now have the key to the time control box.

Then the management had a craze for 'time and motion' studies. They were going to decide what the 'average' man could do at an 'average time of day' and we were all to work to that. They forgot men aren't machines. What if a bloke is feeling a bit off colour, or if he's tired at the end of a shift? Management seemed to think he could keep going at the same pace the whole eight hours of a shift. They did agree in the end to allow six minutes for going to the toilet!

Something we all hated was the 'blue-eyed' system. That meant favouritism by the supervisors. There is no real skill in car assembly, so anyone can do any of the work. The supervisors used to choose their own favourites for the easy jobs, and make sure they had any overtime that was going. You had no chance of earning overtime at all if you been branded as a trouble maker. We got over that by making them put everyone's name in a hat.

Some really dirty tricks have been played by management. We had a first rate steward, and of course he was a pain in the neck to the supervisor. To get his own back he planted a component in the steward's rucksack and tipped off the security men at the gate to search it. Luckily one of the lads saw what was happening. He reported it and stuck to his story. The supervisor was questioned all night, and in the end he confessed.

We've got management where we want them

now. They know that if they go against us shop stewards we will call everyone out on strike at once. The car industry has never done so well as at present, and the company can sell everything it makes. A long stoppage would cost millions. Management will give into us every time rather than have that happen.

A labour relations executive in the motor industry, 1970s

There is a lot of trouble in the motor industry today. We have a crisis of authority. The ordinary worker just does not know whom he should obey. Is it his trade union, his employer or his shop steward?

This company recognized Trade Unions just after the war, but it made it plain it would negotiate only at national level. I must say that most trade union leaders are reasonable men, so it is usually possible to come to some understanding with them. What happened, I'm afraid, was that the shop stewards became powerful and since then we have had nothing but trouble. It is impossible to deal with many of these people. There is one of them I know whose idea of negotiation is just to shout abuse. When he has finished he registers a 'failure to agree'.

What the unions say they want is 'mutuality'. That would mean management and trade unions sitting down and deciding between them how the factory should be run. They do not realize it would be the ruin of the company. In management we know what we must do to make a profit, and we must be free to make the decisions. If there are no profits, there will be no company and no jobs. There will be little point in arguing about how this factory should be organized after it is closed.

There has been a lot of fuss about time and motion and 'speeding up'. The men on the line seem to think we want them to sweat blood, but it is not that at all. We know the factory is capable of producing a certain number of cars, and all we are asking our workers to do is to make a good continuous effort and produce them. But will they? Not a bit of it. Our company has a factory in Belgium, identical to this one. They make half as many cars again as we do. If they fail to reach their high production targets, which is very rare, they are worried and disappointed. Here, if we meet our much lower targets, we are very surprised. The whole difference is in the attitude of our workers.

Most of the trouble comes from sheer laziness. They arrive late, they sleep on the night shift, they

A shop floor meeting with a shop steward.

have days off. There is even organized laziness. We found a group of ten workers who paid into a pool every week. Each one took Friday off in turn, and collected the pool so that his wages did not suffer.

There is a lot of dishonesty amongst the workforce, and an alarming amount of stealing goes on. Once we caught a gang using the components of our car indicators to make flashing lights for their Christmas trees. A man will even go through the gate with an accumulator on his handlebars, hidden under his cycle cape. We had to dismiss one security officer, not because he didn't do his job, but for catching too many thieves. The shop stewards insisted that we should get rid of him.

There has been a lot of hooliganism among the young workers. Some of them once took the skin from a supervisor's orange, filled it with bostic and then watched him peel it. This was harmless enough, but they found they could make bostic bombs and we had flames twenty feet high. We had to plead with the shop stewards to make them stop it.

As well as high jinks there was deliberate sabotage. We had to lay some men off a while ago, and as we hoped until the last minute we might avoid it, we didn't tell them until the Friday afternoon. Their answer was to go down a line of cars, scratching the paint with knives.

The biggest menace, though, is Communism. I know a lot of the stewards are Communists. They admit it quite openly. To them a strike is not about pay, conditions or any other problem. It is a method of weakening the economy of this country. They have glib tongues, however, and the ordinary workers follow them like sheep.

I hate to say it, but I honestly think the only answer to our problems will be a bad recession. Every year more and more foreign cars come into this country, and before long we shall be unable to sell our own. Factories will close, there will be massive unemployment and those still working will tremble for their jobs. Perhaps then the ordinary workers will realize where these agitators have led them. I hope we will then be able to sack a few communist shop stewards and restore discipline. Workers must work and management must manage. It is the only way to succeed.

Industry: Conclusion

In recent years factories have begun to use automation. This means that instead of people controlling machines, computers do so. At first there was a problem because computers were very large and expensive. Since the invention of the silicon chip, however, they can be quite small and reasonably cheap. Also, the machines which the computers control have become more complicated. For example, 'robots' can assemble motor cars.

It is likely that during the 1980s machines and computers will take over many of the boring jobs in factories. People will no longer have to work on production lines, and this is probably good. But if machines do all our work for us what are we to do? A boring job is unpleasant, but for many people unemployment is worse.

In the early nineteenth century we saw that the handloom weavers were angry because the power looms were putting them out of work. In fact, the new machines created more jobs than they destroyed. Whether our modern inventions will do the same remains to be seen.

Questions

1 Where were Britain's most important industries in the nineteenth century?
2 Why was it possible to start many new inventions in the South of England in the twentieth century?
3 What are the advantages of mass production?
4 What grievances did the workers in the motor industry have? What did they do about them?
5 What complaints did the labour relations executive have about the men in his factory?

The new British car assembly line; robot controlled.

Work Section

1 Homes and Families

1. Find examples of houses built at different periods in your area. Also look through books on architecture. Which style do you like and why?
2. Why do many rich people today like to own a house that was built in the eighteenth century? What must be done to modernize such a house?
3. In what ways might it have been pleasant to be the child of the eighteenth century squire? In what ways might you have found him annoying?
4. What is your opinion of the Yorkshire clothier as a man and as a parent?
5. Do you think the barrister's daughter was right to feel frustrated? What would you have done in her place?
6. How did the ending of the domestic system affect working class families? (See chapter 9, page 104 and Chapter 10, pages 118–19.)
7. When Disraeli wrote his novel 'Sybil' he gave it the sub-title 'The Two Nations'. Why is this a good description of nineteenth century England?
8. Are the differences between rich families and poor families greater today than in the nineteenth century, or are they less?
9. Is it better to live in an unhealthy slum and be happy, or to live in a clean, new house and be miserable?
10. Should a young wife depend heavily on her mother? Why are working class girls more likely to do this than the daughter of wealthier parents?
11. Contrast your own childhood with that of other people brought up in the eighteenth and nineteenth centuries. Do you think you are more fortunate? Why?
12. Contrast modern parents with those of the eighteenth and nineteenth centuries. What differences are there? Are there any similarities?
13. Why do fathers have much less authority today than they had in the past? Do you think this is good? Could it be one reason for the increase in crime?
14. Why is it sometimes necessary to demolish blocks of flats which may be no more than fifteen years old?
15. What do you like and dislike about your home and the area in which you live? What improvements would you make?

2 Leisure

1. Why do you suppose people of the eighteenth century enjoyed blood sports? Does anything fill a similar need today?
2. How was Beau Nash, a man from an ordinary family, able to make nobles obey him?
3. How much credit can Beau Nash have for the splendid eighteenth century buildings of Bath?
4. In what ways are modern games better organized than those of the eighteenth century? In what ways are things just as bad?
5. Why have certain people in all ages found pleasure in violence and cruelty?
6. Why do we forbid cock fighting and bear baiting today, but allow fox hunting, pheasant shooting and deer stalking?
7. Consider the changes in football, horse racing and boxing between the eighteenth and nineteenth centuries. Compare them with the changes in keeping law and order. (See Chapter 5.)
8. What do you think the locksmiths of Wolverhampton should have done to enjoy life more?
9. Do you think people should be more active in their leisure time, and not sit back and be entertained? Give reasons for your answer.
10. How are modern holiday camps different from those of the 1950s?
11. How important was it for the Earl of Plymouth to kill his fox, or for the pigeon fancier to win his races? How important is it to win at any sport?
12. How many of the sports mentioned in this chapter involve animals? Can you think of any others that do? Is it right for people to use animals for sport?
13. Since leisure is so important today, why do people object to being out of work? (See Chapter 4.)
14. What are your own leisure activities? What do they tell you about yourself?

3 Education

1. What is your opinion of the Rector who founded the Charity School?
2. Imagine it is possible for you to meet a child from an eighteenth century Charity School. Write a discussion you and this child might have about your schools. How are they different? Are they similar in any ways?
3. What did the government do to help education in the nineteenth century?
4. What is your opinion of 'payment by results'? What would be the arguments against having a similar system at the present day?
5. What part did religion play in education in the eighteenth and nineteenth centuries? What part does it play today? Should it be more important, or less?
6. Write a discussion which the Grammar School French mistress might have had with the Secondary Modern Woodwork teacher.

7 Do you think it is better to have comprehensive schools than grammar and secondary modern schools? Why?
8 What changes have there been in your school in recent years? What, if any, are planned for the future?
9 In the past, what people outside the schools have tried to influence them? Why? What people do so today? Why?
10 In what ways are schools today more ambitious for their pupils than those of the eighteenth and nineteenth centuries? Why do you suppose this is?
11 What attempts have been made at various times to give children from poor families an education?
12 List the main changes that have taken place in education since 1700. Which do you think was the most important? Why?
13 Are there any school buildings in your area that date from the nineteenth century? Are they still used as schools?
14 Talk to your parents and grandparents about their school days. Compare them with each other and with your own.

4 The Care of the Poor

1 Which people were unhappy with the poor law in the late eighteenth century? Which of them, do you suppose, were pleased with the Poor Law Amendment Act of 1834?
2 Do you think the people who tried to reform the poor law in the early nineteenth century were well-meaning or just cruel? What went wrong with their plans?
3 What have been the different ways of dealing with unemployment over the centuries?
4 Read through the chapter and find examples of how the poor have been treated a) kindly b) unkindly. Why do you suppose the treatment of the poor has varied like this?
5 Why was it difficult for someone who was unemployed to keep his self respect in the eighteenth, nineteenth and early twentieth centuries? Is it easier today?
6 Why are most of us anxious that people who are capable of working should do so?
7 Is 'work dodging' common today? How would you stop it without causing hardship to those in real need, as happened after 1836?
8 Shall we ever have as much respect for people who are unemployed as we do for those who are in work?
9 What steps have the poor and unemployed taken at various times to improve their own lot? Do you think they could have done more or acted differently?
10 How would you use your time if you were unemployed? How would you prevent unemployment affecting you as it did some of the people in this chapter?
11 It is sometimes said that schools should prepare their pupils for unemployment rather than work. Do you agree? In any event, how could this be done?
12 Is it better to be unemployed than do dull, repetitive work?
13 What changes in industry are helping to make people unemployed today? (See Chapter 10.)
14 Is 'work sharing' a good idea? It would mean that instead of some people being unemployed, everyone would work a few hours less each week. Who is likely to be against such a scheme? Can you see any difficulties with it?

5 Law and Order

1 What did the eighteenth-century constable have in common with the overseer of the poor? (See Chapter 4.)
2 Where do you think John Fielding and Sir Charles Rowan would have agreed? Where would they have disagreed?
3 How has the treatment of criminals changed since 1700? Are these changes for the better?
4 How has the treatment of young offenders changed since 1700? Are there any other changes you would like to see?
5 Consider the treatment of criminals and of the poor in the nineteenth century. What similarities do you notice?
6 Consider education, care of the poor and law and order. What part, if any, did the government play in all of these in the eighteenth century? Who was mainly responsible?
7 How did people show their dislike of the police in the eighteenth and nineteenth centuries? Why do many law abiding people dislike the police today? What is your opinion of the police force?
8 How would you feel about making a career in the police or the prison service? If you had to take one or the other, which would it be? Why?
9 Are you pleased when you learn that someone especially unpleasant has been sent to prison? Why? What do you hope will happen to him there?
10 Is it possible to punish a man in prison and, at the same time, reform him?
11 How would a number of years in prison affect you? What would you most dislike?
12 'It is not fear of punishment which will deter a criminal, but fear of being caught'. Do you agree?
13 Do you think the 'Bobby on the beat' would be more efficient than the policeman in the panda car?
14 How would you solve the problem of crime today?

6 Medicine

1. What 'quack' remedies are in use today? Why do people believe in them?
2. How did eighteenth-century doctors find bodies to dissect? (See Chapter 2, 'Leisure in the Eighteenth Century'.)
3. Why did vaccination prevent smallpox? What diseases are prevented in a similar way today?
4. Why did Edward Jenner have no scruples about experimenting on James Phipps?
5. Suppose a strange new disease made its appearance today. Do you imagine people would react to it, as the citizens of Exeter did to the cholera?
6. Find out how cholera is carried. Decide which of the measures taken by the people of Exeter would have been effective. Which were a waste of time?
7. When dealing with disease, people in the nineteenth century sometimes did the right things for the wrong reasons. Find examples of this.
8. When Edwin Chadwick tried to put his ideas into practice, many people opposed him. Why do you suppose that was?
9. What experience have you, or members of your family, had of the National Health Service? Were you satisfied with what happened? If not, what do you think went wrong?
10. Why do large numbers of people pay for private treatment? Should this be allowed?
11. Since cigarette smoking is one of the main causes of ill health why does the government not ban it? What drugs are illegal? Why?
12. 'Prevention is better than cure'. What steps have been taken to prevent disease in the past? What is being done at the present? Should more be done?
13. Why might some people be unwilling to admit they have a close relation in a mental home? How could this attitude be changed?

7 Inland Transport

1. In the eighteenth century, what did care of the roads have in common with the care of the poor and the keeping of law and order?
2. Find out more about Thomas Telford and John Macadam.
3. Imagine you are an eighteenth-century farmer. Write a discussion you might have had with a local innkeeper about a plan to 'turnpike' a road in your area.
4. Why did the development of coal mining go hand in hand with the growth of canals and railways?
5. Why were railways more efficient than turnpike roads or canals?
6. What is the main use of our inland waterways today? Do you think they could become important once again, as the roads did?
7. Why is road transport more important than rail transport today?
8. What efforts do British Rail make to attract passengers? Read some of their advertisements to see what arguments they use. Would British Rail make more money if it charged lower fares?
9. What was the last journey of any length which you made in Britain? What method of transport did you choose? Why?
10. Do you think the taxpayer should meet British Rail's losses?
11. What mistakes do you think have been made in the development of our system of inland transport? What changes would you like to see?
12. Why does a transport strike e.g. tanker drivers or railwaymen have such serious results for the whole country? Would similar strikes have done as much damage a hundred or two hundred years ago?
13. Why are many people happy to work many hours, unpaid, restoring old canals?
14. What is the appeal of the steam locomotive? How do people show their enthusiasm for steam railways?
15. Study the growth of the transport system in your area under the headings:— prehistoric trackways, if any; turnpike roads (look for old toll houses and coaching inns as well as consulting your local library) canalized rivers and canals; railways, open and abandoned; road improvements e.g. widening and building of by-passes; motorways.

8 Sea and Air Transport

1. Imagine you are an ordinary seaman on an eighteenth century collier brig. Write a discussion you might have with a sailor on a vessel which trades overseas. Compare your work and the difficulties and dangers you face.
2. Find out what you can about Eddystone Lighthouse and its history.
3. How did the development of the coal industry go hand in hand with the development of sea transport?
4. Why did iron and steel become increasingly important in shipbuilding?
5. Find out more about clipper ships. Where can you see one today?
6. Why did steam ships replace sailing ships in the late nineteenth century?
7. Find out what experiments have been made with sails on large merchant vessels in recent years. Is it likely that sails will once more become important?
8. How did the development of the steamer help Ireland? What services are there across the Irish Sea at the present day?
9. Look in the 'Guinness Book of Records' to find the largest ship ever built. How does she compare with Brunel's 'Great Eastern'?

10 How have sea and air transport helped inland transport at various times? How have they competed with it?
11 Read more about the history of the airship. What attempts are being made to revive it? How could airships be used at the present day?
12 Read about the development of the aeroplane during the two world wars. Why was there more progress in time of war than in time of peace?
13 Should governments be allowed to spend large sums of money on projects like Concorde without first consulting their people? How could an ordinary person judge whether such a project was likely to succeed?
14 Which is the more important, to travel quickly or to travel cheaply?
15 How has the ability to travel quickly and easily made our lives different from those of our ancestors? Is the change for the better?

9 The Countryside

1 At the beginning of the eighteenth century the population of England and Wales was 5½ million. At the end of the century it was 9 million. What would have happened had there been no improvements in farming?
2 Why did farmers plant hedgerows in the eighteenth century? Why are they grubbing them up today?
3 Why did people oppose the enclosure of common land in the eighteenth century? Why would they do so today?
4 Was it right that cottagers and small farmers should suffer for the good of the country as a whole? Give some modern examples where better things for many folk have meant hardship for a few. Can this kind of thing be prevented?
5 Calculate the age of some hedgerows. You pace out 30 yards, and count the different species of bush growing in that distance. The number of species gives you the approximate age in hundreds of years e.g. four species, four hundred years.
6 Why was the period 1850–1870 a 'golden age' for farmers? Why did it end? What other 'golden ages' have farmers enjoyed?
7 How have industry and transport helped farming, at different times? How have they sometimes harmed it?
8 Go through the chapter and list the problems that poor countryfolk have had to face at different times. Look also at Chapter Four 'The Care of the Poor'. Use the information to write the history of a family through several generations.
9 Consider the rich and the poor in the countryside during the eighteenth, nineteenth and twentieth centuries. Why have there always been big differences between them?

10 Do you agree that farmers are spoiling the countryside? If so what should be done to stop them? Is it fair to interfere with the way they make a living from their own land? When you have considered this problem write a discussion a farmer might have with a conservationist.
11 Consider any village you know well. What problems does it share with the Oxfordshire village described in this chapter? What others does it have?
12 Would you sooner live in the town or the countryside? Where would you prefer to work? Give reasons for your answers.

10 Industry

1 How did coal mining and the iron industry help one another? In what other ways has coal been important? (See Chapters 7 and 8.)
2 How did the iron industry help the development of transport?
3 What other examples have you found of industries helping each other, both in this book, and in your own experience?
4 What industries were there in your area in the eighteenth and nineteenth centuries? Have any survived to the present day? What modern industries are there?
5 Find out more about the machines first used in the cotton industry.
6 Read about the development of the steam engine.
7 What work was done by children in farming and industry during the eighteenth and nineteenth centuries? (See Chapters 1 and 9 as well as 10.)
8 What have been the main sources of power? When was coal at its most important? What sources of power do you think will be used in the future? (See Chapters 7, 8, 9 as well as 10.)
9 How have workers suffered in the past because of changes in their industries? What is done for workers who are made redundant today? What else do you think should be done to help them?
10 In the 1950s hardly any of the cars sold in Britain were imported. In 1980 60 per cent of them were. How do you explain this change?
11 Read about the growth of industry in Japan. Why is Japan so successful at the present day?
12 What do you think the factory of the future will be like?
13 Why do some people prefer goods made by hand to those made by machine?
14 What handicraft industries have survived from the eighteenth and nineteenth centuries? Do you think it is important that they should continue?
15 Do you enjoy working with your hands? If so, are you likely to find a job where you can use your skills?

Acknowledgements

The publishers would like to thank the following for permission to reproduce photographs:

Aerofilms, pp. 100, 110, 121; Alison Anholt White, pp. 8, 28, 73 (*left*), 80, 111 (right); Avon County Library, p. 19 (*top*); Barnaby's Picture Library, pp. 37, 59 (*top*), 97, 98; Bath City Council, p. 19 (*right*); B.B.C. Hulton Picture Library, pp. 9 (*top left and right*), 11 (*top left*), 17 (*top left*), 19 (*bottom left*), 23, 30 (*top*), 31, 40, 42, 43, 44, 45, 46, 47, 48, 59 (*bottom*), 64 (*bottom*), 65 (*top*), 66, 68, 71, 77, 79, 101, 118; Bodleian Library, p. 11 (*bottom*); British Airways, pp. 96, 99 (*bottom*); British Leyland, p. 123; Bridgeman Art Library, pp. 17 (*bottom*), 54, 120; Camera Talks ("Art Therapy" film), p. 74; Central Office of Information, pp. 30, 61, 62, 63, 72; Colonial Williamsburg Foundation, p. 64 (*top*); Colour-Rail, p. 86; Devon County Library, p. 69; Ivor J. Dixon, p. 108; Dorchester Museum, p. 112; Mary Evans Picture Library, pp. 9 (*bottom*), 17 (*top left*), 52, 56, 57, 70 (*left*), 76, 95; E. Fattorini, p. 32; Fox Photos, pp. 12, 96; Gavin Graham Gallery, p. 102; Henry Grant, pp. 38, 39, 75; Richard Green, p. 104; Mrs. A. Haynes, Milham Ford School, Oxford, p. 36; Historical Newspaper Loan Service, p. 24; Michael Howarth, pp. 14, 109, 111; Illustrated London News Picture Library, p. 11 (*top right*), 15, 105; Ironbridge Gorge Museum, pp. 115, 131; Judkyn-Pratt Collection, p. 21; Keystone Press Agency, pp. 13 (*top*), 49, 50; M.A.N. Diesel, p. 85; Mansell Collection, pp. 7, 10, 35, 41, 53 (*top*), 58, 113 (*left*); Maritime Museum, pp. 88, 89 (*bottom right*), 90, 91, 92; Roger Mayne, p. 113 (*right*); Roy Miles Gallery, London, pp. 5, 106; K. Mott, p. 26; National Portrait Gallery, p. 18; National Trust, pp. 4, 6; Network, p. 51; Popperfoto, p. 25; Rex Features, pp. 60, 99 (*right*); Ann Ronan, p. 67; Rugby School, p. 20; S.S. Great Britain Project, p. 94; Science Museum, p. 114; Sir John Soane's Museum, p. 55; Peter Speed, p. 33; Tony Stone, p. 84; Tate Gallery, pp. 29 (*bottom*), 93; John Topham, p. 12 (*top*); Trades Union Congress Library, pp. 119, 122; Vision International, pp. 71, 87; Waterways Museum, p. 81; Wolverhampton Art Gallery, p. 103.
Borough of Darlington Museum, p. 83.

Illustration on p. 22 by Graham Humphreys.
The photograph of the Chartist Meeting of 1848 is reproduced by gracious permission of Her Majesty Queen Elizabeth II.
Cover illustrations courtesy of Mary Evans Picture Library, Manchester City Art Gallery, Popperfoto.